T0323692

Cambridge Elements ≡

Elements in Bioethics and Neuroethics
edited by
Thomasine Kushner
California Pacific Medical Center, San Francisco

BIOETHICS, PUBLIC REASON, AND RELIGION

The Liberalism Problem

Leonard M. Fleck
Michigan State University

Shaftesbury Road, Cambridge CB2 8EA, United Kingdom

One Liberty Plaza, 20th Floor, New York, NY 10006, USA

477 Williamstown Road, Port Melbourne, VIC 3207, Australia

314–321, 3rd Floor, Plot 3, Splendor Forum, Jasola District Centre,
New Delhi – 110025, India

103 Penang Road, #05–06/07, Visioncrest Commercial, Singapore 238467

Cambridge University Press is part of Cambridge University Press & Assessment,
a department of the University of Cambridge.

We share the University's mission to contribute to society through the pursuit of
education, learning and research at the highest international levels of excellence.

www.cambridge.org
Information on this title: www.cambridge.org/9781009078054

DOI: 10.1017/9781009086684

First published 2022

A catalogue record for this publication is available from the British Library.

ISBN 978-1-009-07805-4 Paperback
ISSN 2752-3934 (online)
ISSN 2752-3926 (print)

Bioethics, Public Reason, and Religion

The Liberalism Problem

Elements in Bioethics and Neuroethics

DOI: 10.1017/9781009086684
First published online: August 2022

Leonard M. Fleck
Michigan State University

Author for correspondence: Leonard M. Fleck, fleck@msu.edu

Abstract: Can religious arguments provide a reasonable, justified basis for restrictive (coercive) public policies regarding numerous ethically and politically controversial medical interventions, such as research with human embryos, preimplantation genetic diagnosis, or using artificial wombs? With Rawls, we answer negatively. Liberally reasonable policies must address these controversial technologies on the basis of public reasons accessible to all, even if not fully agreeable by all. Further, public democratic deliberation requires participants to construct these policies *as citizens* who are agnostic with respect to the truth of all comprehensive doctrines, whether secular or religious. The goal of these deliberations is practical, namely, to identify reasonable policy options that reflect fair terms of cooperation in a liberal, pluralistic society. Further, religious advocates may participate in formal policymaking processes as reasonable liberal citizens. Finally, public reason evolves through the deliberative process and all the novel technological challenges medicine generates for bioethics and related public policies.

Keywords: public reason, political liberalism, religious restraint, bioethics, medical research

ISBNs: 9781009078054 (PB), 9781009086684 (OC)
ISSNs: 2752-3934 (online), 2752-3926 (print)

Contents

1 Introduction

The United States Supreme Court currently (early 2022) has under consideration the case of *Dobbs* v. *Jackson Women's Health Organization*. The issue before the court is whether or not Mississippi's ban on abortions after fifteen weeks is constitutionally permissible. It is seen by many commentators as a threat to the sustainability of the 1973 Supreme Court decision, *Roe* v. *Wade*, which legally permitted abortion as a matter to be decided between a woman and her physician up to the twenty-fourth week of a pregnancy. The basis for the decision was that this was a constitutionally protected right of privacy. The legal implication of this decision was that states were not allowed to ban abortion before the twenty-fourth week of a pregnancy. This meant that all existing state laws that banned abortion prior to that time were immediately invalidated. The competing claim by opponents of abortion under any circumstance was that abortion was murder. That claim could make legal sense only if the fetus was legally considered a person from the moment of conception (as many advocates for a right to life would assert). However, the Court declared that the status of the fetus was a "metaphysical" question beyond the ability of the Court to adjudicate. If *Roe* v. *Wade* were overturned, that would mean that each state would be free to establish whatever restrictions it wished regarding abortion. In essence, a constitutionally protected right of privacy would have been profoundly diminished.[1]

The Guttmacher Institute[2] estimates that if *Roe* v. *Wade* were overturned, twenty-six states would certainly or likely ban all abortions. What would justify the abolition (in twenty-six states) of such a fundamental right? What state interests would justify coercively intruding into the physician–patient relationship? States regulate in all manner of ways many health-care interventions, very few of which generate the passionate opposition we have seen with the broad legalization of abortion. Why is abortion different?

Before saying anything more, let me make clear to the reader that this Element is not about abortion as such. Abortion is only the tip of the proverbial iceberg. The rest of the iceberg consists of all the novel medical technologies that have emerged over the past sixty years or so that have occasioned vociferous opposition largely from religious groups for religious reasons, that is, reasons embedded in a religious belief system. Some quick examples would include physician aid-in-dying, CRISPER-cas9 gene editing of embryos, selling sperm or ova, surrogate mothers, in vitro fertilization, preimplantation genetic diagnosis (PGD), contraception, medical research with human embryos, human cloning, gender reassignment surgery, the use of anencephalic infants as organ donors, federal research funding for enhancing human life expectancy, and the development and implementation of artificial wombs. In a liberal pluralistic society, I doubt that anyone could justifiably object to expression of opposition to any of these practices either within some specific religious community or in any of a number of casual social conversations. All of these conversations in a liberal society would be protected free speech, legally and politically speaking. However, it is a very different matter when societal decision-makers responsible for making public policies that will bind everyone put in place policies that would ban or severely constrain all of the these practices for reasons that are essentially religious or narrowly ideological. This is what has come to be known as the problem of "religion in the public square."[3]

The broad question framing this Element is whether religious arguments can provide a reasonable justified basis for restrictive (coercive) public policies in a liberal, pluralistic society. The narrower question we will address is whether religious arguments can provide a reasonable, justified basis for restrictive (coercive) public policies with respect to a broad range of innovative (but ethically and politically controversial) medical technologies, such as those listed earlier. My short answer to that latter question will be negative. However, that just raises the question of whether advocates for these religious arguments are being treated illiberally and disrespectfully. Are they being reduced to the status of second-class citizens? I will also answer that question in the negative. On the face of it, however, it does seem as if religious beliefs and commitments are banned from the public square, thereby devaluing those ideas. Is that true? Is that fair? Is that reasonable?

Wolterstorff[4] asks why religious reasons should not be permitted to compete for public attention in the public square in the same way that secular ideas compete in the public square. After all, he argues, if those religious ideas are so unattractive and so unreasonable, they will never win any significant allegiance in the public square. On the other hand, if those ideas are reasonable and compelling, as in the case of Dr. Martin Luther King's efforts to see enacted robust civil rights legislation, then they most certainly deserve to be heard in the public square and enacted in legislative bodies.[5] There is no doubt in my mind that Dr. King's rhetoric is elevating and ennobling. However, the real question is whether religious rhetoric that can attract the support of a democratic majority does in fact *justify* the public policies to which that rhetoric is attached from the perspective of a liberal, pluralistic democratic society.

I remind the reader that religious rhetoric has been used to support slavery, miscegenation laws, and laws that would severely punish homosexual behavior among consenting adults.[6] In relation to my specific bioethical focus, I can imagine a majority of Americans persuaded by religious rhetoric endorsing the banning of all abortions, including all medical interventions or research that involved the creation and destruction of embryos, such as IVF, PGD, gene editing of embryos, genetic research with embryos, and so on. Such an outcome, I would argue, represents something illiberal, unreasonable, and undemocratic, something entirely lacking justification from a Rawlsian liberal perspective. These concerns are what prompt Rawls (and me) to ask: "How is it possible for those affirming a religious doctrine that is based on religious authority, for example, the Church or the Bible, also to hold a reasonable political conception that supports a just democratic regime" (Rawls, 1996, xxxix)? It would be unreasonable and illiberal to expect that these religious individuals would give up their religious commitments in order to live peacefully in a democratic society. But it would be equally unreasonable and illiberal to permit specific religious beliefs and values to legitimate public policies that would outlaw or severely restrict access for everyone to some range of novel medical technologies judged unacceptable from the perspective of that religious doctrine.

2 Rawlsian Political Liberalism

In the remainder of this Element, I wish to defend an essentially Rawlsian position with regard to the role of public reason in addressing the questions I have raised. I will give considerable attention to explicating and justifying the role of public reason in addressing from a public policy perspective the controversial medical technologies that are the focus of bioethics today. I will be defending "an essentially Rawlsian position" as opposed to explicating it as accurately as possible Rawls' texts. There are gaps and deficiencies in Rawls' position that have been the focus of critical attention (discussed in Sections 5.1–5.4). I hope to remedy those gaps and deficiencies.

2.1 What Is Political Liberalism?

Rawls characterizes his own position as *political* liberalism, as opposed to philosophic liberalism. Philosophic liberalism represents what Rawls describes as a "comprehensive doctrine." Marxism, Platonism, Hegelianism, Thomism, libertarianism, and so on would all represent comprehensive doctrines as well because they all claim to offer a complete world view informing adherents of what is real, what is true, and how we ought to live (as individuals and in society). All religions are also seen by Rawls as representing comprehensive doctrines for the very same reasons. We should add that the same is true for atheism. Rawls says that his political liberalism is agnostic with regard to all these comprehensive doctrines. That is, he neither asserts nor denies any of the truth claims asserted by any of these comprehensive doctrines. He adds that his own political liberalism is not advancing any truth claims; it is instead a *practical* doctrine designed to address complex, fundamental political problems in a liberal, pluralistic, democratic, tolerant society. This may sound odd to many readers since philosophers generally seem to be making truth claims regarding their philosophic theories. Rawls, however, has this practical focus for his political liberalism: What is it that *we must do* in creating public policies that are reasonable regarding ethically controversial novel medical interventions, such as artificial wombs or PGD? What sort of regulations of these novel technologies is congruent with our understanding of fair terms of cooperation and the most fundamental principles of a liberal society? No doubt, those practical judgments will rely upon numerous truth claims. But those truth claims will be of a scientific variety or common-sense social experience, not metaphysical or epistemological theories.

2.2 Political Liberalism: A Key Problem

Rawls does not see himself advocating for some utopian society to which we ought to aspire. Instead, he takes as his starting point the most fundamental values that are already embedded in our liberal culture. Rawls asks, "How is it possible that there may exist over time a stable and just society of free and equal citizens profoundly divided by reasonable religious, philosophical, and moral doctrines?"[7] In other words, if there are these deep religious and moral disagreements regarding the political foundations of our society, how can we possibly expect to live peaceably with one another? As noted, this challenge for Rawls is a practical political problem, not a matter of irreconcilable competing ideologies. What is necessary is a shared conception of justice "specifying fair terms of cooperation between citizens regarded as free and equal, and as fully cooperating members of society over a complete life, from one generation to the next."[8] How will we get to those fair terms of cooperation?

2.3 Public Reason

Those fair terms of cooperation will require reasoned and informed discussion respecting everyone as free and equal citizens, which is to say that the agreements are entered freely, not as a result of manipulation or coercion. Those agreements will express their shared and public political reason. "But to attain such a shared reason, the conception of justice should be, as far as possible, independent of the opposing and conflicting philosophical and religious doctrines that citizens affirm."[9] Rawls describes what he refers to as "public or political reason" as "freestanding," which is to say that it is not dependent upon any metaphysical or philosophical or religious conceptions.[10] Public reason is the method for solving fundamental public problems that *citizens as citizens* (as explained in Section 2.7) must embrace to address fundamental political problems. It may be thought of as a common language or a common perspective. Public reason appeals "only to presently accepted general beliefs and forms of reasoning found in common sense, and the methods and conclusions of science when these are not controversial."[11]

Public reason does not come "fully stocked" with specific beliefs and values in the way that Catholicism or libertarianism or Marxism would come "fully stocked." However, that does not mean public reason is contentless. The content of public reason accrues over decades in response to a range of political problems that are the object of political controversy. This is a point to which a number of Rawlsian commentators have not given sufficient attention. Rawls writes: "Whether public reason can settle all, or almost all, political questions by a reasonable ordering of political values cannot be decided in the abstract independent of actual cases . . . . For how we think about a kind of case depends not on general considerations alone but on our formulating relevant political values we may not have imagined before we reflect about particular instances."[12] This is precisely what we will be doing in the latter portions of this Element as a way of testing the adequacy and utility of public reason.

As noted in Section 2.3, Rawls sees public reason drawing its content from the liberal democratic culture already endorsed and lived by its members. It is a matter of social construction for which there will be many reasonable (not true) answers. What are being constructed are the basic structures of society, constitutional essentials, and responses to political problems related to those constitutional essentials. Keep in mind that constitutional essentials are not created and fully specified at a single point in time. What would the right to privacy have meant to the Founders of the United States at the Constitutional Convention in 1787? What would our Founders have to say about the scope of procreative liberty, including the use of PGD or the creation of artificial wombs? Were these medical interventions constitutionally protected, perhaps subject to various degrees of regulation but not justifiably banned outright? The very asking of these questions makes clear that our Founders had given no thought to these questions but that we would need to be engaged in ongoing construction of reasonable responses to these controversial questions.

2.4 A Liberal Society

A liberal society is committed to respecting the equal freedoms and equal rights of all its citizens. A liberal society recognizes that many reasonable values may be used to construct a fulfilling life for any individual. In a liberal society as a society no value is superior to all other values in all social contexts, nor is there some hierarchy of values that a liberal society embeds in all its social policies and social practices. A liberal society, for example, will encourage its citizens to make more healthy dietary choices rather than less healthy choices (and may offer guidance in this regard), but a liberal society will not ban all fast-food restaurants, nor will it observe or regulate the frequency with which its citizens choose to consume fast food each month. A liberal society will allow advocates for healthier living to promulgate their views through multiple forms of social communication. A liberal society will allow both vegetarians and meat lovers to advocate for their respective views, though this must be done in a way that does not violate the equal political rights and liberties of their competitors. Likewise, neither side may make claims for their dietary recommendations that are not supported by reliable scientific evidence. Thus, if vegetarians were to become a majority in our society, they could not justifiably use their majoritarian status to ban the production, sale, and consumption of meat products. No imaginable rationale could justify such a policy without undermining profoundly the liberal character of our society. Meat lovers are not violating the rights of anyone else, nor are they undermining some significant public interest, nor does their behavior make for a substantially less just society.[13] Hindus might be offended by the widespread consumption of beef in our society, and both Jews and Islamists might be offended by the widespread consumption of pork. However, banning the production, consumption, and sale of beef and pork to satisfy these religious beliefs would again be profoundly illiberal.

Compare our comments regarding meat lovers and vegetarians to our regulation of pharmaceuticals. The vast majority of pharmaceuticals are available to the public only with a medical prescription. Despite the fact that we are a liberal society committed to protecting the scope of individual freedom, virtually no one objects to limiting access to prescription drugs as illiberal or unreasonable. Likewise, the manufacturers of these drugs are not free to make these drugs available through normal market mechanisms. Instead, numerous regulations devised by the Food and Drug Administration must be met by these manufacturers that are aimed at assuring the safety and efficacy of these drugs. Again, virtually no one objects to these regulations as being illiberal or unreasonable. However, there are these health practitioners who are called "Naturopathic doctors." They are advocates for allowing the healing capacities of the body to work on their own to restore health without introducing foreign substances into the body. Here is a sentence from one of their websites: "Conventional doctors may prescribe you a medication to suppress your symptoms, which never truly helps the body heal and resolve the health issue."[14] What I want to emphasize is their assertion that conventional medications "never truly help."

This will strike most of us as a seriously misleading exaggeration. I pass over that for the moment.

What I ask you to imagine is that the naturopaths develop a very persuasive message, so powerful that they are able to get legislation passed that bans the manufacture and distribution of all the pharmaceuticals with which we are currently familiar. Such legislation would clearly be illiberal and unreasonable. It would lack scientific justification; it would reflect instead an ideological position that was outside the bounds of public reason. However, what should also be noted is that naturopathic medical practices are not inherently dangerous to health, and consequently, a liberal society would not be justified in banning these practices. By way of contrast, adult Christian Scientists may put their own lives at risk by refusing effective and necessary medical care in accord with their religious beliefs, though they may not put at risk the lives of their children in similar circumstances. A liberal society justifiably intervenes to protect those children in such cases. These are conclusions endorsed by public reason.

2.5 Freestanding Public Reason

What precisely is public reason? Why must public reason be "freestanding," divorced from all comprehensive doctrines? Rawls points out as a fact of our political culture that it is *reasonably pluralistic*. This is not a temporary state of affairs. It is a permanent feature of any democratic culture. What this implies is the potential for disagreement regarding numerous political problems, perhaps very widespread and consequential political problems. Some specific resolution may be congruent with some comprehensive doctrines and incongruent with others. In either case, a resolution will mean the formulation and legitimation of a public policy that can be coercively enforced by government, likely to the disadvantage of adherents of the incongruent comprehensive doctrine. What Rawls recognizes is that the use of the coercive powers of government must be justified to everyone who might be affected by the use of those coercive powers. This is what Rawls refers to as the liberal principle of legitimacy. He defines that principle as follows: "Our exercise of political power is fully proper when it is exercised in accordance with a constitution, the essentials of which all citizens as free and equal may reasonably be expected to endorse in the light of principles and ideals acceptable to their common human reason."[15]

It is important to be clear regarding what Rawls is both affirming and not affirming in this passage. First, that constitution may be thought of as the embodiment of a political conception of justice, which is freestanding, not a product of any comprehensive doctrine. Second, that constitution is a product of our common reason or public reason, again, unencumbered by any comprehensive doctrine. The "our" in this case are free and equal citizens seeking fair terms of cooperation. These are the most basic elements of a liberal society. If some individuals think of themselves as being superior to everyone else in their status as citizens, as having more rights or stronger rights than everyone else, then those individuals are unreasonable and are not *liberal* members of society. Liberal members of society are committed to fair terms of cooperation, which is essentially a matter of reciprocity. Rawls writes, "Fair terms of cooperation specify an idea of reciprocity: all who are engaged in cooperation and who do their part as the rules and procedures require, are to benefit in an appropriate way as assessed by a suitable benchmark of comparison."[16] Third, cooperation is not coercion. Liberal citizens respect one another as free and equal members of this society. Consequently, we rely upon persuasion to achieve mutually acceptable agreements regarding the policies that will bind us all. We foreswear all forms of manipulation and deception in the shaping of public policies because such practices are contrary to mutual respect. That brings us to our fourth point.

2.6 The Rational and the Reasonable

We recognize one another as being both rational and reasonable as citizens. These too are essential to the foundations of a liberal society and what it means to be free and equal as citizens. To be reasonable means we have the power to propose fair terms of cooperation and to abide by those terms, so long as others do the same. To be rational means we have the moral power to have a conception of the good. Rawls emphasizes that free citizens are not necessarily tied to any particular conception of the good across their entire life. "Rather, as citizens, they are seen as capable of revising and changing this conception on reasonable and rational grounds, and they may do this if they so desire."[17] Rawls goes on to say that citizens may convert from one religion to another or give up any specific religious identity entirely. For purposes of political justice, such individuals remain the same persons that they were before. In other words, their identity *as citizens* would not have changed in the least. Strong advocates for various religious identities may believe that those identities are nearly immutable and that those identities must pervade every aspect of a person's life. Such individuals are free to make such choices for themselves, though I will argue, as Rawls would argue, that such a choice cannot infuse their distinctive political role *as citizens* in a liberal society. This is really the heart of the debate about religion in the public square.

2.7 The Role of Citizen

What does it mean to behave *as a citizen* for Rawls? Rawls writes, "Public reason is characteristic of a democratic people: it is the reason of its citizens, of those sharing the status of equal citizenship. The subject of their reason is the good of the public: what the political conception of justice requires of society's basic structure of institutions, and of the purposes and ends they are to serve."[18] Though this may sound harsh and insensitive, public reason must not be contaminated by the private goals or expectations of specific religious groups or advocates for some comprehensive doctrine. The focus of public reason must be public interests, interests that each and every citizen in a liberal society has. Recall that public policies always have a coercive element built into them. That element of coercion can be justified only if the goal of the policy is to protect or enhance some public interest, including basic human rights.

Roman Catholics comprise approximately 22 percent of the US population. If Roman Catholic lobbying groups were especially astute and effective in getting national legislation approved that would ban all artificial contraceptive methods in accord with Roman Catholic doctrine, such legislation would be egregiously illiberal and unreasonable. No obvious public interest would be served by such a policy. On the contrary, both liberty interests and privacy interests would be public interests that would be violated by such a policy. Assume the US Supreme Court agreed with that judgment and overturned the law. Could ardent Catholics claim to be justly aggrieved, that this decision represented disrespect for their religious beliefs? Could they claim that this decision effectively "gave permission" to less ardent Catholics to use artificial contraceptives, contrary to Church doctrine?

At this point we would ask those ardent Catholics to put their Catholicism in the back of their minds and reflect more thoughtfully on their demands for contraceptive policy from the perspective of citizens in a liberal, pluralistic society. We could encourage them to become reflective in this way with the following thought experiment: Imagine that ardent Islamists in the United States combined with ardent Hindus in the United States to secure the passage of legislation forbidding the manufacture, sale, and consumption of pork and beef products, per the requirements of their respective religions. Meat-eating ardent Catholics would vigorously object to having such a policy, though they could just as readily be accused of being disrespectful of the religious beliefs of the Islamists and Hindus. They could argue that such a policy was not justified by any public interest and that this policy would violate their privacy rights and liberty rights. Of course, they would be correct in that judgment, just as non-Catholics would be correct in objecting to the Catholic anti-contraceptive policy. In order to voice those objections, however, and expect that they would be taken seriously, these individuals could not be speaking from a Catholic perspective. Such a perspective would not reflect public reason. The same would hold true for the Hindus and the Islamists. If adherents of these different religious perspectives wished to live peacefully with one another in a liberal, pluralistic society, then they would have to come to fundamental political agreements with one another *as citizens*, not as members of some religious group.

Being a citizen is a distinct social role with its own rights and responsibilities. It requires putting aside other social roles and identities that might not be compatible with the role of being a citizen charged with seeking reasonable fundamental political agreements. Citizens as citizens are responsible for articulating the details of a political conception of justice, especially in relation to emerging biomedical technologies that are seen as being ethically and politically controversial. Some of that controversy might be attached to specific religious beliefs. Those elements of the controversy will need to be settled within the confines of specific religious communities. From the perspective of a liberal pluralistic society, that would be both rational and reasonable. Some members of that religious community may disagree with some proposed resolution of those controversies within the community. They have the right to voice their disagreement, to act in accord with their disagreement (practice contraception, eat pork), and to exit the community if the disagreement is profound enough. These are rights that they possess *as citizens* within the broader liberal community that embraces all these distinctive religious voices. Specific religious communities might not wish to explicitly acknowledge those rights, but those rights are real and enforceable by the larger liberal community. No religious community has the legal right to imprison any of its adherents for uttering heretical statements or for seeking to persuade others to leave that community. Such individuals may be publicly admonished; they may be shunned by other members of the community. They may be excommunicated. But they cannot have any of their liberty rights or property rights forcefully taken away.

Ironically, those very same rights that some religious groups may wish to violate are the very rights that protect the integrity of all these religious communities from invidious discrimination and related political violence. The legitimate expectation within a liberal society is that the adherents of these different religious traditions will all accord one another mutual respect, though, again, this is an expectation that applies to these religious adherents *as citizens*. Within their respective houses of worship, they may all wish to affirm that they alone have the "one, true faith" while everyone else is wallowing in heresy and ignorance. Noteworthy is that no court would ever accept as a legitimate case for adjudication one church seeking an injunction against another church for "falsely asserting" that they alone were the one true religion.

3 Religion and Liberalism

Some number of religious writers will claim that it is both illiberal and unreasonable to expect that an individual's religious identity would somehow be sequestered from every other social identity an individual might possess, most especially their identity as a citizen. Wolterstorff writes,

> "It belongs to the religious convictions of a good many religious people in our society that they ought to base their decisions concerning fundamental issues of justice on their religious convictions. They do not view it as an option whether or not to do so. It is their conviction that they ought to strive for wholeness, integrity, integration in their lives."[19]

Along these same lines, Vallier writes,

> "To split an identity is to corner-off the social space in which individuals can act in accord with their own judgments. Thus, political theories that split identities prevent citizens from acting on their convictions in some vital domain of life. Since activity in that domain (it is assumed) is of great important, restraint threatens to alienate citizens from their values and principles."[20]

Most radical of all are the views of the Islamic scholar, Sayyid Qutb. These views were summarized by Paul Berman[21] and reported in an essay by Wolterstorff.[22] Qutb is opposed to what he refers to as the "schizophrenia" of modern political life, that is, the separation of the secular and the sacred. Qutb is opposed to the idea of Islam being confined to a private emotional life and religious ritual. He wants Islam to dominate every area of secular life. In summarizing Qutb's views, Wolterstorff writes, "Shariah must be reinstituted as the legal code for all of society, so that God's law can once again hold sway for all of everybody's life. Only then will divinity and humanity be once again united."[23]

3.1 The Limits of Religious Integrity

However, some reflection will show these "integrationist views" do not represent a position most religious advocates would ultimately wish to defend. Imagine a physician, psychological therapist, marriage counselor, or high-school teacher using their professional position to proselytize for their religious views. It is difficult to imagine a Roman Catholic or evangelical Protestant accepting with equanimity such behavior by a devout Islamist in any of these roles. Their expectation would be that the Islamist's religious identity be left outside the clinic or classroom, given the needy and subservient position that patients and students would be in typically. Moreover, all the social roles mentioned here have a public identity inherent in the role. These are individuals serving a public interest in education or health care in which a public investment has been made. Patients and students are seeking the best advice and most reliable knowledge available, not something skewed by the provider's religious identity.

The example given here is of something very overt that might annoy a patient and that could be tuned out. However, covert insertions of one's religious identity would be even more problematic in these professional contexts. Imagine a couple that has recently discovered they are both carriers of a cystic fibrosis mutation, which means there would be a 25 percent chance of having a child with cystic fibrosis. They seek help from their obstetrician, who, unbeknownst to them, was a strong advocate for religious reasons of a right to life position. He encourages them to either seek to adopt children or else accept the results of normal sexual intercourse, reminding them that God would not impose upon them a burden they could not bear. He does not mention to them the option of IVF and PGD because that procedure would necessarily involve the creation and destruction of many eight-cell embryos, each of which would have been denied their right to life. What I readily acknowledge is that this obstetrician, as a matter of conscience, does not have a moral obligation to provide IVF and PGD as an alternative way to have children without cystic fibrosis. However, this obstetrician would have the ethical and professional obligation to inform this couple of this option because his skills and knowledge as an obstetrician were a product of substantial public investments for public purposes. He would not have the right to withhold access to those public goods for his personal religious reasons. The same would be true if he allowed his partisan political identity to infect his professional identity as a physician in such a way that he provided a higher standard of care to patients who shared his political identity than to those with a different political identity.

One of the distinctive features of a liberal society is that its members can assume many different social roles or social identities. Many of these social roles are very informal (parent, grandparent, sibling, neighbor, friend) and are defined by many different cultural understandings. Others are much more formal with very clearly defined rights and responsibilities (physician, judge, nurse, professor, mayor, financial consultant, police officer, engineer, priest), which establish in a public way expectations, limitations, obligations, and permissions. Parents and priests have rights and responsibilities with respect to the religious education of children. However, in the formal social roles identified here, and dozens of others that could be named, engaging in some form of religious education directed toward students or clients or patients or the criminally accused would be regarded as inappropriate (at least), sometimes absolutely forbidden (imagine a religious physician seeking the deathbed conversion of a professed atheist patient).

3.2 Religion and the Legislative Role

The reader will notice that I did not mention "legislator" or "citizen," which is where the crux of our problem is. All the other social roles I mentioned affect only a very limited clientele specific to those roles. Individuals in those client groups generally have the freedom to choose some other physician or financial consultant or religious leader or professor. However, legislators, whether state or federal, are responsible for creating public policies that potentially affect everyone within that jurisdiction. Of special concern would be policies that would punish citizens who violated those policies, especially if those punishments involved loss of freedom for years in a prison environment. Likewise, policies that permitted discrimination of various forms (jobs, housing, health care) against socially disfavored groups would also have to be a matter of special concern, as would policies that constrained various liberty rights that did not threaten any public interest. In all of these cases we will argue that it would be egregiously illiberal and unjust if specific religious commitments had been built into these policies as the justifying basis for these policies. Legislators in a liberal, pluralistic society would have violated their role responsibilities if they endorsed such policies. Likewise, citizens as citizens in a liberal, pluralistic society would also violate their responsibilities as liberal citizens if they advocated for such policies, no matter how sincere their religious beliefs, no matter how important those beliefs were in defining the meaning of their lives.

The expectation in all these cases, from a Rawlsian perspective, is that legislators, judges, and public administrators as well as citizens would confine their advocacy for specific public policies to within the bounds of public reason. This leads to the challenge that Rawls readily recognizes: "Why should citizens in discussing and voting on the most fundamental political questions honor the limits of public reason? How can it be either reasonable or rational, when basic matters are at stake, for citizens to appeal only to a public conception of justice and not to the whole truth as they see it"?[24] We turn again to the advocates for a more robust role for religious beliefs and religious values in the creation of public policies. We will consider the main arguments in support of their positions as well as their criticisms of the limitations imposed by public reason.

Their most general complaint is that public reason liberalism excludes or marginalizes persons of faith from public political life.

3.3 Public Reason, Integrity, and Religious Commitment

We return to the "integrity" objection. Michael Perry[25] has argued that if individuals are forced to bracket their religious convictions, that is, completely privatize them, then that represents the annihilation of one's very self. If individuals are forced by liberal societal expectations to withhold from public debates about important political matters their deepest religious values, then they are presenting a false self in public according to Perry. In that respect, they have lost their integrity. Philip Quinn[26] contends that the principles of restraint proposed by public reason liberals exclude religious advocates from public discussion. Quinn wants to defend what he calls an inclusivist ideal. He writes, "The inclusivist ideal is more attractive than its rival because, being less restrictive, it allows all citizens to express themselves and their deepest values more fully in the political sphere and is apt to mitigate the problem of alienation from the political."[27] Vallier is another strong defender of the integrity objection. He writes, "One traditional reason to endorse liberalism is that it *preserves* the integrity of all citizens. If liberals are committed to *frustrating* integrity, then this is cause for alarm, for if liberalism unjustifiably restricts integrity, a crucial rationale for liberalism is undermined."[28] Finally, Kent Greenawalt objects to the way in which public reason liberals privilege secular reasoning over religious reasoning in the political arena, thereby reducing religious advocates and their views to second-class status.[29]

If we talk about integrity at this very abstract level, it is difficult to imagine some form of liberalism justifiably failing to protect the integrity of the beliefs and values of individuals. However, if we descend from this very abstract level to more concrete examples of integrity, we will readily see that there are politically and ethically reasonable and unreasonable forms of integrity. Criminals can be committed with integrity to a life of crime. No liberal society can tolerate that sort of integrity. As we noted in Section 3.1, there have been religious groups that have defended on religious grounds various forms of racism, homophobia, sexism, child abuse, and any number of other practices that would clearly violate the basic rights of others, contrary to the most fundamental commitments of a liberal society. They may claim that this is a matter of religious integrity, that these various beliefs and practices are integral to their worldview (and the worldview everyone else ought to adopt). It is obvious that these sorts of hateful beliefs and practices cannot be tolerated in a liberal society, at least in the public square, no matter how integral these beliefs might be to some religious worldview.

I think we do need to emphasize that we are talking about the public square where we address basic matters of public policy as citizens. Consequently, no matter how embarrassing or politically challenging it might be, we do need to allow religious congregations that refuse to admit non-whites or individuals who are gay "for religious reasons" to do just that. In so acting they are not violating anyone's rights because no one has the right to force their way into a religious congregation if that congregation is unwilling to accept them. We might be inclined to think such congregations are merely exercising their privacy rights. However, that would be incorrect. Country clubs and various social groups, such as fraternities and sororities, or the Elks or Masons or Odd Fellows, have excluded blacks and other minorities from their membership prior to the civil rights movement.[30] These are all private organizations that nevertheless offer public benefits and opportunities for their members, which is why they have all been legally compelled to give up their discriminatory behavior. By way of contrast, religious organizations have been given special political protections in this regard, though the limits of those protections continue to be the focus of some political disagreements. Thus, a religiously affiliated hospital may not refuse to care for HIV+ patients because of the behavior related to their becoming HIV+, but a Catholic school may legally fire a teacher who is openly gay simply because they are openly gay and judged to be engaged in a lifestyle contrary to Catholic doctrine. This last statement might be open to reasonable disagreement. From one liberal perspective, we might see the firing of this teacher as a violation of their rights, unjust discrimination. From another liberal perspective, we might see a Catholic school and its choice of who to employ as protected by our understanding of religious freedom, and respect for the integrity of that religious belief system. These decisions are made, we might say, in the privacy of that religious system. Invoking that argument, however, elicits objections from religious advocates who are opposed to confining religious commitments to some private realm. They want their religious commitments to be an integral part of public life and a public political culture.

Again, I would argue that this "privacy" objection is an exaggeration regarding the limits a Rawlsian liberal society would place upon the expression of religiously motivated political views in the public political culture. To illustrate, imagine some coalition of religious groups picketing several public schools where it is known some of the teachers are gay and demanding that all those teachers be fired because they are gay. A liberal society will permit such peaceful demonstrations as protected free speech. But Rawls would argue that those demonstrators are open to justified moral criticism for advocating the illiberal view that those teachers ought to be fired because they are gay. This is what Rawls refers to as the expectation of "civility" in a liberal society.[31] We can turn this scenario around. We can imagine a group of Protestant protesters picketing public schools and demanding that all Catholic teachers in those schools be fired because they believed the first allegiance of those teachers would be to the Pope rather than the US constitution. Catholics would be rightfully upset by such a situation, though they would understand that they would legally and politically have to allow that picketing. However, they could also judge such behavior as illiberal and uncivil, and be open to justified ethical criticism for that reason. That is, these picketers would be flawed liberal citizens. A point I want to emphasize is that in both these cases we are in the public square. That is, a liberal society will do nothing to prevent these protesters from engaging in these public actions that have some religious motivation behind them, even though the behavior itself is ethically objectionable.

Consider another situation. A preacher from the pulpit denounces the "gay lifestyle" as contrary to the will of God and worthy of condemnation to eternal hellfire. That same preacher could say those same things on a street corner, and a liberal society will protect that behavior as free speech (the assumption being the speech is not designed to elicit violent behavior aimed at gay individuals). In that respect, the "integrity" of those religiously rooted beliefs has not been confined to heavily cordoned off private space.

Let us add one more element to this scenario. Our preacher is denouncing from the pulpit a specific gay politician and demanding that members of the congregation not vote for that individual. This is behavior that a liberal society can rightfully outlaw. In the United States, for example, religious organizations have tax-exempt status on the grounds that they are doing various sorts of public good, that is, addressing the needs of the poor, visiting the sick in hospitals, and so on. These organizations, however, are specifically forbidden from engaging in partisan politics, especially working for or against a specific politician or specific political party. The penalty for violating this directive is loss of that tax-exempt status. The justification for this penalty is that the religious organization is doing something that represents a narrow private interest rather than a public interest. Consequently, a public subsidy is no longer justified. Religious organizations are free to proselytize in the public square, that is, the public political culture. This would not warrant withdrawal of the tax subsidy because they are simply adding to the numbers of individuals in their congregation available to do some public good. There are literally hundreds of things that religiously motivated individuals can do in the public culture that contribute to some public good and that do not violate the rights of others in society. From this perspective, it hardly seems warranted to say that religious beliefs and values have been unjustly or illiberally privatized, or that an individual's religious integrity has been unjustly or illiberally threatened or corrupted.

3.4 Religious Integrity and Physician Aid-In-Dying

Here is a critical question: What is respect for religious integrity supposed to mean in a liberal, *pluralistic* society when we must address through public policy some especially controversial issue such as permitting physician aid-in-dying? Perhaps some in our society imagine that all religious individuals would be profoundly opposed to permitting this practice. That is completely imaginary. In the real world, individuals from many different religious perspectives would be completely supportive of this practice, while others would completely condemn the practice, and still others would be scattered all along the spectrum between these poles. On the assumption that all these individuals would justify their particular view by appealing to their favored religious scripture, religious tradition, or revered religious leader, the result would not be a policy conversation. Instead, it would be a policy cacophony. They would all be talking past one another. The result would be a policy stalemate.

Such a policy stalemate would have three major consequences with respect to the liberal foundations of this society. First, the social capacity for thoughtful and effective democratic deliberation would have been eviscerated, at least with respect to important policy issues that elicited substantial opposition from some significant religious perspective. The very same outcome would almost certainly occur with respect to a broad range of controversial bioethics issues related to emerging medical technologies, such as abortions achieved through Plan "B," or the use of PGD to identify embryos free of specific genetic disorders, or the use of human embryos in medical research to better understand the earliest stages of embryonic development, or the use of artificial wombs, or doing whole-genome sequencing (WGS) at birth, and so on. How is a public conversation supposed to evolve if participants are isolated in irreconcilable comprehensive religious perspectives? What is supposed to count as evidence for or against any point of view if appeal is to radically different sources of evidence? A productive conversation will require shared standards for evidence and reasoning, which is what Rawls' notion of public reason is intended to provide.

Second, a stalemate is not a neutral outcome with respect to the contending perspectives. With respect to physician aid-in-dying, a stalemate would mean that the practice would remain illegal. That would mean that the coercive powers of the state would be used to fine or imprison anyone who provided physician aid-in-dying to a desperate terminally ill patient. This is not an outcome that would be warranted by public reason because there would not have been any reasonable form of democratic deliberation. In turn, that means advocates for the legalization of this practice would be denied access to the benefits of this practice for reasons that they could not accept as reasonable because those reasons were attached to some comprehensive religious perspective they did not endorse. Whenever a policy decision needs to be made with respect to a controversial medical practice, it is clear that proponents of some alternate policy choice will be disappointed. However, if that policy decision is the product of a fair democratic deliberative process governed by public reason, the losers in the process can at least accept as reasonable the outcome of the deliberative process because the reasons that justified that outcome would be reasons they understood to be legitimate reasons, that is, reasons not rooted in some comprehensive doctrine. This is what is referred to in the relevant literature as the "accessibility" requirement. In the situation I described this is precisely what is not the case. The reasons that would be the basis for continuing to outlaw physician aid-in-dying would be rooted in some comprehensive religious doctrine that would not be reasonable or accessible to those who rejected that comprehensive religious doctrine. Consequently, additional discussion would be pointless, especially if that discussion were initiated from some alternative comprehensive perspective.

Third, the stalemate we described would be an illiberal outcome. Pluralism is integral to any legitimate form of liberalism. Multiple reasonable values will be relevant to any significant policy decision. In addition, the interpretation and application of those values to any specific policy decision will have to respect what Rawls refers to as the "burdens of judgment."[32] Consequently, the public deliberative process will often be about balancing and suitably interpreting these reasonable values as reflected in a concrete policy decision. Trade-offs will have to be made. It will rarely be the case that some policy will be justifiably rigidly exceptionless. For example, we want to protect the public from drugs that might be unsafe or ineffective. I assume the reader recognizes that there are degrees of safety and effectiveness. We could insist that no drug would be available to the public if it were not absolutely safe and perfectly effective. The result would be the availability of virtually no prescription drugs, and the consequence of that would be enormous preventable human suffering and premature death. Consequently, we create rigorous systems for testing experimental drugs so that we have considerable confidence that these drugs are very safe and very effective. At that point we could insist that no drug would be released to the public that had not already met these rigorous standards. If we did insist on that, then we would have to forego permitting "compassionate use" of these drugs by desperate patients facing death with no alternative therapies for their disease other than one of these experimental drugs. That feels cruel and heartless. However, these are desperate patients who might not realize the risks of using one of these experimental drugs might result in a fate worse than death. This is a tug of reasonable values.[33] A caring society will be responsive to these patients and protect them from very bad decisions (though libertarians who are strong advocates for expansive right-to-try laws will regard this as being excessively paternalistic). Hence, we devise a set of rules and recommendations for judging the risks and benefits of compassionate use with respect to specific patients in specific clinical circumstances. The result will be a pluralism of reasonable responses, often adjusted by actual experience with one policy variation or another. This is a response congruent with the foundations of a liberal society.

If we return to our physician aid-in-dying example and the stalemate created by conflicting responses from different comprehensive religious perspectives, the result is clearly illiberal, that is, making absolutely illegal physician aid-in-dying for reasons embedded in a very conservative comprehensive religious view. There are no exceptions; there is no balancing of competing values that might give significant weight in some circumstances to compassionate concerns for patients faced with a cruel death. What we need to ask is whether from the perspective of public reason there is a compelling reasonable justification for this exceptionless policy regarding physician aid-in-dying. If there is not a compelling public interest that would require such a restrictive policy, then we ought to respect the right of individuals to make such decisions for themselves with the advice of their physicians. Everyone can readily recognize the potential for mistakes and abuse in this situation, that is, desperate patients, tired caregivers, greedy relatives, and so on. Reasonable regulations can be crafted (and have been crafted) to address these concerns. No doubt this more reasonable policy would be contrary to the deepest commitments of some religious groups. However, this policy has no coercive effects on any of these religious groups. These groups are free to inform their members that a permissive policy regarding physician aid-in-dying is contrary to their presumed religious commitments. They could threaten members with excommunication if those individuals advocated for a more liberal policy.

To return to an earlier point, if opposition to physician aid-in-dying is regarded as being essential to the religious integrity of members of this congregation, a liberal society will allow and protect the right of members of this community to hold these beliefs and to act on them so long as those actions did not threaten the basic rights of either members of that community or individuals outside that community. Thus, they would be free to picket outside a hospital in which terminally ill patients had the option of physician aid-in-dying. Note that in this respect they would have access to the proverbial public square. But they would not have the right to threaten with bodily harm physicians or other health professionals who were participants in that practice. Likewise, if a member of their congregation were dying of an extraordinarily painful cancer in their home, and if that individual now decided they wanted access to physician aid-in-dying, and if other members of that congregation became aware of their change of heart, those other members would not have the right to block access to that home to prevent a physician from entering that home who intended to provide aid-in-dying. Such behavior would be clearly illiberal because the member of that congregation who has had a change of heart clearly has the right to such a change of heart *as a citizen in a liberal society.*

Our hypothetical religious group might object that they are being treated illiberally because of these constraints imposed on their behavior. However, the most fundamental value in a liberal society is a commitment to *equal concern and respect* for all members of that society. What our hypothetical religious group must keep in mind is that their rights of protest and free speech are protected by this liberal society, and that protection includes their being protected from any form of physical intimidation, including destruction of their property, by any other political group that might strenuously disagree with their point of view. Again, that protection extends to them *as liberal citizens* in this society who are expected to be respectful of all other liberal citizens and to express their views in reasonable ways. Such expectations do not threaten their religious integrity, nor do such expectations reduce them to second-class citizens in this society.

To be clear, Rawls is not advocating that various *religious* perspectives be subject to some range of behavioral and rhetorical constraints. Rather, whatever constraints legitimately applied to religious comprehensive perspectives would also apply to all nonreligious comprehensive perspectives. Thus, atheists would not have the right to disrupt religious services in some church or synagogue because they believed with Karl Marx that religion was nothing more than opium for the masses. This would be a clear violation of the rights of those religious groups who were peacefully worshipping. Atheists would be free to advocate for their views in many different ways through the public culture of a liberal society.

3.5 Religion, Public Policy, and the Restraint Requirement

It is hard to imagine Kantians or utilitarians or Thomists engaging in any violent form of political behavior. However, it is easy to imagine Kantians and utilitarians and Thomists having very different views with respect to the ethical or political legitimacy of physician aid-in-dying. This might result in vigorous argumentation at philosophy conferences or other public settings where such issues might be debated. Various religious voices could be part of these debates as well. In all these cases Rawls would not be insisting that participants in these cases bracket their comprehensive views and only speak with the voice of public reason. The primary reason for this broad permissiveness is that no specific piece of legislation is "on the table" for serious consideration, either legislatively or administratively. Consequently, participants in these public discussions are under no obligation to refrain from appealing to their comprehensive positions. However, it is a very different matter when very specific legislation is being considered for possible enactment. In that situation, participants are legitimately expected to speak *as citizens*, that is, with the voice of public reason, not from within any comprehensive framework. Certainly, this is the expectation Rawls has for individuals in legislative or judicial or public administrative roles, including staff connected to these policymakers. Further, if there are public hearings, then individuals invited to testify, perhaps representing some relevant expertise, would also be expected to offer their contributions *as citizens*, not as advocates from within some comprehensive doctrine. What about broader public engagement? What is the role of rational democratic deliberation with regard to very specific pieces of proposed legislation? I would argue that to the extent such deliberations have a formal character tied in some specific way to a particular piece of legislation participants ought to be speaking as citizens with the voice of public reason. This would be in contrast to less formal public discussions that might be randomly organized.

A number of religious advocates (Wolterstorff, Eberle, and Perry) object to what they refer to as the "restraint requirement" which they see public reason liberals imposing on religious individuals who wish to offer various religious considerations to justify some favored coercive public policy, such as a policy which would forbid medical research involving human embryos. They will contend that this represents an unjust privileging of secular reason over religious reason. The restraint requirement may be seen as being epistemically problematic, or ethically problematic, or politically problematic. Eberle, for example, sees that requirement as being epistemically problematic. He contends that "religious claims, although controversial, are no *more* controversial than are many moral and factual commitments *essential* to healthy political decision making and advocacy."[34] Eberle goes on to claim that any responsible citizen will have to support whatever her favored coercive law might be with some rationale that many of her fellow citizens will find unacceptable and arbitrary. It does not matter whether that rationale is religious or secular. The point is that the coercive force of that law will apply to these other citizens who will clearly feel coerced, which is to say that they will feel that their moral and political rights will have been violated. Eberle's point, contrary to Rawls' expectation that public reason would be more likely to yield broad agreement, is that there will be persistent disagreement whether the rationale for some specific coercive law is religious or secular. Consequently, some portion of the citizenry will feel their moral and political rights will have been ignored or violated by whatever rationale is offered to justify some specific coercive law. Assuming Eberle is correct in describing that outcome, he would conclude that insisting that only an outcome congruent with public reason (secular reason)[35] is acceptable would in fact be illiberal and arbitrary.

3.6 Fallibilism and Public Reason

How should a public reason liberal respond to Eberle? Is public reason fallible? Of course, public reason is fallible. Is public reason in practice peppered with deep disagreements regarding an appropriate policy response in specific circumstances, such as permitting medical research using human embryos? Of course, public reason is peppered with such disagreements, in part because of what Rawls has described as the burdens of judgment, which are an inextricable feature of our scientific, ethical, and political life. Is this a conclusion that supports Eberle's argument? NO!

Science and medicine in practice make mistakes with respect to what we believe we know. However, the virtue of the actual practice of science and medicine (and public reason) is that we have methods for recognizing those mistakes and correcting them. Sometimes those mistakes can be recognized and corrected relatively quickly. At other times, it might take years or decades to correct those mistakes, as evidenced by the history behind civil rights legislation. However, there are widely agreed upon methods for resolving these disagreements when these are matters of scientific fact or forging acceptable compromises when disagreements have a normative character. To illustrate, how is it possible for the continents to move around the globe? That seems to be utterly beyond belief. Nevertheless, the theory of plate tectonics explains both how that is possible and how that has happened and is continuing to happen. The scientific evidence in support of this theory is compelling. No doubt there are millions of individuals who refuse to believe this is true. Few of these individuals have the capacity to understand the science that supports this conclusion, which is to say that their denial of this conclusion and the supporting evidence is unreasonable. Likewise, 13 percent of Americans refuse to believe that we have landed men on the moon. That too is unreasonable. However, how are we supposed to judge that any particular religious belief is unreasonable?

Advocates for any particular religious belief generally believe those beliefs are true, often infallibly true. Still, the fact is that other religious advocates belonging to a different religious group will reject what others regard as infallible truth. Christians, of whatever stripe, will see the world and political life in radically different ways from Islamists, of whatever stripe. We saw earlier that Qutb would want Sharia to be the basis for civil and criminal law. What would we imagine might convince Qutb, or any of his followers, that this would be a terrible mistake, that Sharia did not reflect the will of God? I cannot imagine any empirical evidence or compelling rational argument that would have that effect. What would convince proponents of Sharia that women ought to have equal political rights with men? Again, I cannot imagine any empirical evidence or compelling rational (ethical or political) argument that would have that effect. This is why Rawls would describe comprehensive religious views, such as Qutb's, as being unreasonable.

There might well be an internal rationality associated with Qutb's views, meaning that theologians in that tradition can engage in (internally) rational arguments with one another, in much the same way that Roman Catholic theologians can engage in rational argument with one another. However, those internally rational methods for addressing theological disagreements have no utility for justifying the choice of controversial public policies with coercive implications when those policies must apply to a population with hundreds of diverse religious, philosophic, and ideological perspectives. This is the reason why Rawls contends we need a freestanding public reason as the primary basis for justifying coercive public policies. As noted already, reasonable disagreement will be an integral feature of public reason in practice. However, those reasonable disagreements can be resolved (often) through the skillful use of public reason. Rawls recognizes that public reason will have no utility for advocates of unreasonable comprehensive doctrines, such as Qutb. However, it will be useful and accessible for advocates for a broad range of reasonable comprehensive doctrines, and, in that respect, its rationality is not limited internally in the way in which the logic of most theological perspectives would be internally limited. Consider an illustrative example.

3.7 Public Reason and Research on Embryos

Should we have a public policy that would absolutely forbid any medical research with embryos? We have in mind embryos that are less than fourteen days beyond conception. What considerations would be offered in support of such a restrictive policy? Advocates for a right to life view would contend that the embryo was either a person or a potential person. In either case, the embryo would have a right to life, that is, a right not to be killed. The obvious follow-up question would be: What makes us think the embryo is a person? What is visible under a microscope is a ball of cells that displays none of the traits that we would typically associate with entities we readily recognize as persons. At that point, the advocate for a religious perspective would claim that the embryo has a soul, a spiritual substance that made that 200-cell entity a person. How can a liberal advocate for public reason engage with those religious advocates?

3.7.1 Embryos as Potential Persons

Public reason advocates could say that there is no scientific evidence for the existence of a soul at conception. However, that will generate the retort that we are being guilty of privileging secular reason over religious reason. A better response might be to call attention to the animist beliefs of most of the natives in the Arctic. Those animists believe that some form of a soul energizes everything that exists, not just plants and animals, but rocks and lakes and mountains.[36] Right to life advocates enjoy all sorts of meat products that require killing animals, along with healthful salads that require ripping up or cutting off plants in the prime of their life, not to mention destroying natural objects to build our highways and cities. Right to life advocates would give zero credibility to any of these animistic beliefs, which is an obvious privileging of their religious perspective over that of the animists. Importantly, right to life advocates would not alter any of their mundane social practices out of respect for the views of the animists. This could be described as epistemic arrogance, in contrast to the epistemic humility for which Rawls is an advocate. Rawls states that from the perspective of public reason, a democratic citizen as citizen should simply be agnostic with respect to any of these religious truth claims. If everyone is agnostic for purposes of creating public policy with respect to the full range of religious claims, that is, claims that cannot be verified by either the methods of science or common experience, then we create public space in which we can engage in potentially productive public conversations. In so doing, we are not disparaging anyone's religious beliefs, nor are we saying that any religious belief is more worthy of credibility than any other religious belief.

Philosophers tend not to be especially religious. Some have tried to contribute to the debate about the status of the fetus from a rational nonreligious perspective. Friberg-Fernros,[37] for example, has contended that from the moment of conception an embryo is a rational substance with a right not to be killed. He readily concedes that no embryo or fetus exhibits *first-order rationality,* but they do have *second-order rationality,* which is the capacity to develop first-order rationality at some point in the future. This would seem to be something that can be verified by science and experience. The DNA of the human embryo, in contrast to the DNA of any other animal, does have the capacity to bring about a being with all the rational capacities we associate with persons with the full panoply of moral and political rights. Here we have something that can, in principle, be discussed using the resources of public reason.

The obvious critical question regards the status of entities that can be described as *potential* persons. Do potential persons have actual person rights? If so, it would be clearly wrong to destroy embryos for purposes of scientific research, no matter how valuable we might believe the results of that research might be. However, I am fond of shocking my students with this assertion, "I am potentially President of the United States." I am more than thirty-five years old, and I am a natural born American citizen. Those are the only two requirements for being a potential president. Still, it seems perfectly clear that I have no actual presidential rights. I do not have a right to the use of Air Force One; I do not have a right to FBI protection. Only the actual president of the United States has those rights. To further justify this point, a common example in the bioethics literature is a story about a researcher working in her lab with her five-year-old daughter running around the building. In the lab is a tank with a thousand eight-cell embryos in frozen nitrogen. A fire breaks out. The researcher only has enough time to flee the lab if she either finds her five-year-old daughter or saves instead the tank with the thousand frozen embryos (Lovering,[38] Simkulet[39]). What is the ethically correct choice to make? Asking this question of any number of genuinely religious individuals will typically result in affirming that the researcher must save her daughter. But if we really believed that those embryos, perhaps intended ultimately for implantation and gestation, were really persons in exactly the same sense as that five-year-old girl, then it seems the ethically correct response would be saving a thousand persons rather than one person. In reality, virtually no one will endorse that conclusion. That seems to confirm the view, ethically and politically, that one actual person has actual rights that trump any number of rights we might wish to ascribe to potential persons in the form of embryos.

3.7.2 Embryos Are Not Selves

This line of argument might not always be perfectly convincing to some of my students. What might be in the back of their quasi-scientific minds is that from the moment of conception a unique individual is present who is gradually emerging. In other words, if we ask the question "When did 'I' come to be?" they would contend that happened at the moment of conception. Again, I likely shock them when I assert that "I" was never an embryo. I explain that neither I, nor any of them, can be thought of as being identical with their DNA, certainly not at the moment of conception. "I" am a very rich entity, filled with memories and thoughts and emotions and hopes and numerous rational capacities, none of which were there at the moment of conception (or for many months thereafter). "I" came to be only very gradually, mostly in the early months and years after birth, mostly through complex processes of human interaction, including the acquisition of language and the coming to be of self-consciousness. This is a story that the biological and social sciences would affirm today, at least in this broad outline. What this means is that if the biological origins of my future possible self as an eight-cell frozen embryo were lost in that lab fire, I would *not* have been destroyed. I would not have died in a fire. Simply speaking, "I" would not have been there to suffer that fate.

3.7.3 Embryos and Medical Research

This brings us back to the question of whether it would be liberally justifiable to ban all medical research with human embryos. If the justification for such a ban were the claim that these embryos are persons with the same moral and legal rights as you and I, that would not be a reasonable claim, as suggested by the prior arguments. That is, this is not a claim that could be rationally endorsed through public reason. This does not prevent any religious group from attributing a "sacred" status to human embryos. It is noteworthy that Ronald Dworkin, as a political liberal, has sympathy for this claim. The fact of the matter is that these embryos are a human life form, perhaps worthy of having attributed to them some sort of distinct moral status, unlike the embryos of any other species.[40] What might be the practical import of that with regard to the issue of using human embryos in medical research?

It is ethically significant that the embryos used in medical research come from leftover embryos generated in the course of IVF. There are approximately 500,000 such eight-cell embryos that exist in a frozen state in liquid nitrogen. In theory, these excess embryos are available to the couples who produced them for future pregnancies (or for current efforts to achieve pregnancy since, on average, three tries are required for a successful pregnancy). As a practical medical matter, it is necessary to produce these excess embryos because there are risks associated with both the drug needed to induce hyperovulation in a woman and the surgical procedure that harvests these excess ova. The result, however, is the creation of these 500,000 embryos in liquid nitrogen, the vast majority of which will never be used to achieve a pregnancy. After five years or so, these embryos may be removed from the liquid nitrogen and discarded, per an agreement with the couples that created those embryos. These are the embryos that will be used in various sorts of medical research, again, with explicit permission from the couples who generated these embryos.

The ethically significant fact is that all these embryos are slated for destruction. The ethical argument is that use of these embryos for research aimed at saving future possible fetuses and children represents the achievement of an important human good that could not otherwise be achieved. Alternatively, those embryos are simply wasted with no human good achieved. Among the research objectives for which these embryos are being used would be achieving a better understanding of embryonic development during the first twelve days after conception. Why might that be important, not just from the perspective of medical science, but from the perspective of right to life? It is estimated that more than 60 percent of conceptions that occur fail to result in the birth of a baby.[41] The vast majority of these are lost without a woman even knowing that a conception had occurred. It is believed that most of these are a result of a failure to implant in the womb. It is speculated that there is some genetic flaw in the embryo that results in this failure to implant. Depending upon what is learned from this research, it may or may not prove possible to intervene in some way to prevent this loss. The only way to know one way or the other is to do the research.

What I assume is that most reasonable people with an adequate appreciation of medicine and the biological sciences would regard this as a reasonable research objective. In other words, this is a reasonable public interest that does not involve violating the rights of anyone. Further, no competing public interest would speak against or outweigh this public interest. No doubt, some individuals would find the destruction of embryos for this purpose offensive. However, if that offensiveness is very much subjective and very much embedded in a comprehensive doctrine, that would not be sufficient to justify a law that would outright ban the research, at least from the perspective of liberal public reason. If we reflect for a moment, we will quickly realize that an enormous amount of behavior can be regarded as being offensive by some social group which, if banned, would result in a society the Taliban would endorse but that would hardly be recognized as a liberal society, for example, a bikini bottom made in the pattern of the American flag. Having said that, we return to our embryos.

A liberal society committed to public reason has no reasonable basis for ascribing to embryos personal status and a full set of basic human rights. Does that imply that embryos can be used in any way at all for any purpose that does not violate someone's rights? No! Could medical researchers appropriate three hundred frozen embryos without seeking explicit permission from the couples that generated those embryos? No! That is a clear violation of several rights had by those couples. Could those researchers appropriate embryos for which a couple had failed to pay storage fees for two years, perhaps claiming that those couples must have abandoned those embryos? No! It would be liberally legitimate and reasonable to require that those researchers still secure explicit permission from those couples. Could these researchers pay couples to create embryos that might have genetic features that were of special interest to these researchers?[42] Alternatively, could these researchers pay $500 per embryo to a couple that was reluctant at first to surrender their frozen embryos for medical research? Could a liberal society justifiably forbid such transactions in either of these cases? We do not permit individuals to sell their votes or to sell body parts, such as a kidney for transplant purposes. How analogous are these latter transactions to our proposed transactions related to frozen embryos?

I am not going to try to offer an answer to this last question in this Element. This is the sort of question that would have to be addressed through democratic dialogue among citizens as citizens. This is a point to which we called attention earlier, namely, Rawls' comment that these latter questions are not quickly and easily addressed by appeal to some basic political principle. Rather, it will be necessary to pay attention to relevant factual details and what might be called past considered political judgments similar in important respects to the case being addressed. What should be obvious is that it will not be sufficient to assert that these frozen embryos are not persons and have no moral or political rights, thereby intending that should end the discussion. We can consider another example.

3.7.4 The Misuse of Embryos

Imagine a right to life rally seeking to call attention to current debates in the US Supreme Court regarding abortion. Also imagine a protester and his supporters at that rally with a flask that contains one hundred partially frozen embryos which he shows to the crowd. He shatters the flask and stomps all over the frozen embryos to make the political point that he has not violated anyone's rights, and that he could not be charged with mass murder. Some might see this as protected political speech; others might see it as closer to hate speech that is designed more to incite than educate or communicate. Could a liberal society justifiably forbid the use of embryos for pure political purposes? I can readily imagine liberal advocates with regard to abortion endorsing such a restrictive policy, in part because the behavior is uncivil, in part because the behavior is not congruent with norms of democratic deliberation, in part because (following Dworkin) embryonic human life should be accorded some form of moral and legal respect.[43] Again, those points do not end the discussion. There may be many other relevant considerations that would be part of some form of public deliberation regarding the matter among citizens as citizens relying upon public reason.

3.7.5 Embryos as a Human Life Form

Some additional observations are in order. In denying the personhood of the embryo in the aforementioned discussion, no metaphysical claims are being made regarding the embryo. The description of the embryo is essentially a matter of genetic, biologic, and psychological science, which are all part of public reason. If anyone wished to dispute any of the relevant scientific conclusions regarding the embryo, they would have to offer alternative scientific evidence based on the best methods of science. I believe we can affirm as part of public reason that human embryos are a human life form that ought to be accorded some level of moral respect, as opposed to saying with an air of indifference that the embryo is just a clump of cells. This is a moral claim, but it is a *reasonable* (not true) moral claim rooted in scientific knowledge. This might be a more judicious use of language than Dworkin's attribution of "sacredness" or "inviolability" to the human embryo or fetus.[44] What that moral judgment says is that human embryos ought not be treated frivolously, as if they were dirt or rocks, mere things. This is admittedly a somewhat vague moral judgment that will require more fine-grained moral judgments in specific circumstances. Medical research seeking to understand developmental processes regarding embryos for the sake of potential therapeutic interventions is a serious purpose. Further, it is an objective that cannot be achieved without the actual use of human embryos.

3.8 Embryos, Religious Advocates, and an Overlapping Consensus

At this point I want to call attention to what Rawls has to say regarding reasonable and unreasonable comprehensive doctrines.[45] Advocates for reasonable comprehensive doctrines will affirm from within their comprehensive doctrine a political conception of justice, that is, a commitment to equal concern

and respect for all, equal liberties for all, fair terms of cooperation, and accept-
ance of a reasonable pluralism of values. In other words, reasonable citizens
want to live in a society in which they can cooperate with their fellow citizens on
terms that are acceptable to everyone. Reasonable citizens are unwilling to
impose their comprehensive doctrines on others, in part because they realize
there are many ways to live good lives with others.[46] Catholics, evangelical
Christians, Islamists, and atheists as well as utilitarians and libertarians may all
have different reasons for endorsing that political conception of justice. The net
result for Rawls is the creation of an *overlapping consensus*, which is what
ensures a *stable* liberal society with a broadly shared political perspective that
allows for productive democratic dialogue among advocates for these different
comprehensive doctrines.

Again, to illustrate, using my research embryo example, advocates for
a reasonable comprehensive doctrine may regard embryos as having a soul
from the moment of conception and, consequently, having personal status. But
they are mindful of the fact that there is no scientific evidence for the existence
of souls. This is an act of faith, and others might not share that faith. Also, their
faith might be wrong. This is not something that would be psychologically easy
to affirm. But they realize that others have strong faith convictions of various
kinds that they believe are flat out wrong, or just silly, such as the beliefs of the
animists in the Arctic. Likewise, they themselves do experience some cognitive/
faith dissonance when they think about the example of the research scientist
who saves her five-year-old daughter from the fire rather than the canister with
the thousand embryos. They know that they would ethically endorse that
decision, but it is not congruent with their belief in the personal status of
those embryos. Still, they appreciate the fact that their faith is respected in
this liberal society. They are mindful of other societies in which this would not
be true.

Our religious advocates are ethically uncomfortable with the destruction of
the embryos that are used in that medical research. But they appreciate the
ethical legitimacy of the therapeutic goals that are the ultimate justification for
doing that research. In addition, they can imagine that the research might yield
therapeutic benefits that would be of value to future members of their faith
community. That in itself would be a source of some ethical dissonance. Still,
they wonder whether they would condemn a future member of their community
who took advantage of that therapeutic benefit to have a child with a full and
undiminished life expectancy who otherwise might never have been or have
been with a diminished life of significant suffering. They do understand that the
embryos used in the research would ultimately be destroyed. That does alter the
ethical balance in their mind. And they understand enough of the science that

they realize these embryos are not capable of suffering because they have no nervous system. They wish not so many embryos had to be created in the course of offering IVF, but they again understand the medical reasons why that must be so. They might even be aware of the fact that several members of their community have been able to have children of their own because of the availability of IVF. That is something very life-affirming. They also are grateful that those excess embryos are not some sort of public resource that can be simply appropriated by researchers; explicit permission, freely given, must be sought from the couples who created those embryos. They also applaud the policies in this liberal society that would restrict the ethically appropriate use of these embryos out of respect for these embryos as a human life form.

What I have tried to illustrate in the last three paragraphs is the way in which reasonable religious advocates believing in some version of the personal status of the embryo could come to accept as ethically reasonable the use of embryos in medical research. They would see themselves as liberal citizens using public reason (shared reason) to address a complex policy issue. They might have started the conversation, not at all disposed to approve a public policy that would permit the use of human embryos for some range of medical research. But they would have listened respectfully to others with their reasons for wanting to support such a policy. Ultimately, in the scenario I sketched they would have been disposed to approve the policy. However, it could have turned out differently. They might have struggled with trying to figure out how everyone in that conversation might have endorsed the idea that embryos were entitled to some degree of moral respect and then accept (seemingly without any expressed regret) that these embryos would be grown to the several hundred cell stage and then discarded. Still, at the end of the day, they would not have expressed moral outrage with the whole process and its outcome. On the contrary, as liberal citizens they would recognize that those supportive of embryonic research had presented their arguments more persuasively, that all of the considerations that proponents had offered were in fact ethically and politically reasonable, and that in other contexts these religious advocates would have used many of the same arguments and considerations in support of their views. It is in this respect that all these arguments represent broadly shared reasons that constitute public reason.

What I described earlier is what I believe Rawls has in mind when he speaks of an overlapping consensus that establishes the stability of a liberal society. That stability does not require perfect agreement with regard to all significant policy decisions. That is a practical impossibility, just given recognition of the burdens of judgment. Reasonable liberal citizens committed to public reason will still disagree frequently regarding the best policy to adopt for purposes of addressing a specific controversial policy issue. Even if all comprehensive doctrines had been banned from this society and everyone behaved as perfectly reasonable liberal citizens, we would still have intense policy disagreements. That is just the nature of a liberal society committed to respecting value pluralism. In such a society, and with respect to many controversial policy issues, there might not be any policy that in objective terms could be described as the "best" choice. Instead, the more common reality is that there might be several policy options that were somewhat better in different ways than the status quo and other policy options that were somewhat worse.

3.9 Embryos, Religious Advocates, and the Fourteen-Day Rule

I want to return to our discussion of embryo experimentation. Imagine that our religious advocate has come to accept the ethical legitimacy of doing this medical research with embryos. As things are now, the so-called fourteen-day rule applies to this research. Researchers are not permitted to continue to grow those embryos beyond fourteen days. There has been broad agreement on that point for a number of years. The precise reason for that limit might not be entirely clear. Most writers call attention to the emergence of the "primitive streak" in the embryo at fourteen days, that is, the beginning of the nervous system. It is unclear what the ethical significance of that biological fact might be. It has also been noted that we lacked the technical expertise to sustain the embryo beyond that fourteen-day limit. In the past several years a debate has emerged suggesting that the fourteen-day limit should be pushed out to twenty-eight days (McCully,[47] Castelyn,[48] Hyun et al.[49]). Others have expressed vigorous opposition to that idea (Blackshaw and Rodger).[50] Advocates will again call attention to the potential therapeutic value of pursuing that research further. It seems reasonable to suggest that if that rationale was sufficient to justify the first fourteen days, why would it not be sufficient to justify a second fourteen days. Critics (Blackshaw and Rodger) ask where the hard limit would be for this sort of research. Would it be at two months? Would it be at three months? Their concern is that researchers (and society) would be on a slippery slope. I am not going to rehearse all the relevant arguments for and against that idea. The interested reader can follow up my citations.

I am interested in how our religious advocates might react. I can readily imagine that they would express some hesitation regarding this proposed expansion to twenty-eight days. They might be especially concerned about the slippery slope argument. A supporter of extending the research might point out that between day 14 and day 28 the primitive heart begins to form. Things can go wrong there that result in life-threatening cardiac problems for that future possible child. Likewise, during that same period, the nervous system begins to form. Again, neural tube defects can occur during this period that result in either spina bifida or gross brain deformities. The goal of the embryonic research would be to understand how this happens and whether something could be done to prevent these occurrences. Our religious advocates would readily understand and appreciate the seriousness of the research, but they might still ask whether there is some ethically rigid barrier that might prevent researchers from breaching that twenty-eight-day limit. No doubt there would be serious developmental problems that emerge beyond twenty-eight days. So why should that be an absolute limit? Consequently, they might remain reluctant to endorse a policy that would extend that limit. Note that there is nothing "religious" about their concerns in this regard. The very same concern could be voiced by another liberal citizen as a matter of public reason. What needs to be emphasized at this point is that neither of these positions could be fairly described as being unreasonable. There are weighty and liberally acceptable reasons on both sides of this debate. We can imagine that at the end of the day the fourteen-day limit is upheld. Advocates for the extension to twenty-eight days would be disappointed, but they would have to accept the outcome as liberally legitimate. The outcome would not have been corrupted by its justification being at least partially dependent upon some comprehensive doctrine that was outside public reason.

An additional point needs to be noted. Public reason, conceived of as complex methods of reasoning, and public reason, conceived of as the substantive reasons offered in support of controversial policy options, both evolve over time. In that respect, public reason is never complete because the policy problems and public ethics issues that must be addressed are themselves evolving. We saw this point exemplified in a small way in the debate regarding whether the fourteen-day rule should become the twenty-eight-day rule with regard to medical experimentation on embryos. We also identified other aspects of that debate, such as whether couples could be paid (induced) to surrender their frozen embryos for medical research or paid to undergo a medical procedure aimed at generating many embryos for research. The practical reason for the fourteen-day limit initially was the fact that we had no way to sustain the life of an embryo beyond fourteen days. Technological developments since then are what precipitated the discussion of the twenty-eight-day proposed rule. However, a dramatic illustration of where this research is going pertains to the future possible technology of the artificial womb. It might be ten years before this technology is realized; it might be thirty years. The artificial womb would allow for the gestation of a fetus from conception to birth. This is likely to generate a very substantial debate, which has already begun in the bioethics literature. We discuss this in detail in Sections 6.2–6.5.

4 The Restraint Objection

I want to return to what I would regard as one of the strongest objections that religious advocates might direct against public reason liberals. This is the "restraint" or "coercion" objection. Wolterstorff[51] would be one of the more vigorous proponents of this objection. He starts by calling attention to what Rawls refers to as his liberal principle of legitimacy. What makes a coercive law or public policy legitimate (and virtually all laws and public policies have a coercive dimension to them) is that "social cooperation . . . . . is to be conducted so far as possible on terms both intelligible and acceptable to all citizens as reasonable and rational."[52] In another statement Rawls writes: "Our exercise of political power is proper only when we sincerely believe that the reasons we would offer for our political actions – were we to state them as government officials – are sufficient, and we also reasonably think that other citizens might also reasonably accept those reasons."[53] "Only a political conception of justice that all citizens might be reasonably expected to endorse can serve as a basis of public reason and justification."[54]

At this point, Wolterstorff will immediately point out that "there has never been and never will be a society all of whose members agree with all the laws."[55] In other words, what Rawls is proposing is utterly utopian. The point Wolterstorff wishes to make is that if you have all this disagreement in the world regarding virtually every law among citizens who are rational and reasonable, then what is the reason for disallowing religious reasons to be part of the political debate. If all laws and policies have a coercive dimension to them, then religious advocates will potentially be coercively affected by those laws and policies. However, they will not have had a say, or maybe an authentic say [forced to speak citizenese], with regard to the creation of those laws and policies. That is unjust, illiberal, and unreasonable according to Wolterstorff. In effect, he asks how Rawls can claim "everyone" has legitimated some particular law or policy when religious voices and religious reasons have been excluded. Alternatively, religious voices and religious reasons are reduced to second-class status or marginalized relative to "more rational" and "more reasonable" secular voices and reasons.

Wolterstorff contends that Rawls has illegitimately created what he calls a "legitimation pool."[56] Excluded from that pool would be all those individuals who were unreasonable. Only reasonable people are permitted within that pool. Still, there will be all this disagreement, which means that those who disagreed with the approval of some specific law or policy will be coercively governed by that law or policy. That would seem to falsify Rawls principle of political legitimacy unless, as Wolterstorff suggests, "all public reason liberals of the consensus variety propose that one first 'idealize' the members of the legitimation pool by imagining the impairments and deficiencies removed, and then ask whether one has good reason to believe that, with the epistemic impairments and deficiencies removed, all members of the legitimation pool *would* accept one's reason for thinking that the proposed legislation would be a good thing, or *would* at least agree that one's reason is reasonable."[57]

4.1 Rawls and Religious Advocacy

I assume it is obvious that if Rawls' conception of the legitimate use of public reason did look like this it would have no legitimacy whatsoever. Hence, I want to offer a friendlier interpretation of Rawls' views. Recall our starting point: If some social or political groups have been excluded from the creation of coercive laws or policies that will affect them and everyone else, then that law or policy is illegitimate, ethically, and politically. Does Rawls exclude anyone? Yes. Rawls excludes from the deliberative process the unreasonable, those who reject a political conception of justice, that is, those who will not recognize everyone as free and equal, and who will not accept fair terms of cooperation. If individuals see the political process as an opportunity to dominate others, or as an opportunity to advance narrow personal interests at the expense of public interests or the rights of other citizens, then they are not committed to the sort of cooperation essential for a well-functioning democracy. They are not willing to be honest members of a liberal community.

Next, Rawls does not advocate excluding religious advocates from democratic deliberation and the larger political life of a community. Religious advocates, or advocates for any other nonreligious comprehensive doctrine, have access to all the venues that define a liberal political community, as we have already discussed. Still, our ultimate practical problem is the need to address some important policy issue that will involve various sorts of value conflicts. We are mindful of the fact that we are this very large pluralistic political community. We are mindful of the challenges faced in democratic deliberation by the burdens of judgment of which all must be mindful with regard to their personal points of view. We need a common political language with which to communicate with one another, which is a freestanding public reason. If we somewhat very assertively insist on bringing our religious reasons and religious reasoning into that conversation, it will not have the practical effect of advancing the conversation. It is more likely to create an obstacle to a fruitful conversation. In that respect we can be accused of being uncivil for that insistence. As Rawls notes, this may be regarded as a moral failing, relative to what he regards as the responsibilities of liberal citizens. However, no one is forcefully removed from a deliberative body or bound and gagged for seeking to introduce some religious reasons into the discussion.

Next, Wolterstorff emphasizes the fact that in the real world there is always political disagreement at the end of the day because not everyone will see a policy that they were willing to endorse. Does that mean that those individuals are being unjustly, illiberally, and unreasonably coerced by the policy that ultimately won out? No. A fair illustration of what I believe Rawls has in mind is spelled out in considerable detail in this section regarding the use of embryos in medical experimentation. There are all sorts of reasonable reasons that can be offered on both sides of that debate. All of those reasons would be part of public reason. Everyone involved in that debate would recognize that fact, which is why those whose policy preference did not prevail can still accept the results as rational and reasonable, which is to say that they would see neither the deliberative process itself nor the outcomes of the process as being coercive in some objectionable sense.

Next, I want to return to our examples of controversial bioethics issues, some of which might be related to emerging medical technologies. Research with embryos is a good example, as well as stem cell research, physician aid-in-dying, abortion, PGD to identify embryos free of some specific genetic deficiency, or, in the imminent future, genetically altering eight-cell embryos by removing deleterious genes and replacing them with normal copies of those genes. For the sake of argument, I want to assume that all these interventions are given political legitimacy through a process of democratic deliberation and the normal legislative process. I also want to assume, likely easily enough, that all these interventions would be strongly objected to by advocates from various religious perspectives. However, the question I want to raise is this: Is there an ethically and politically problematic sense in which these religious advocates have been *coercively imposed upon* as a result of the liberal legitimation of all these interventions? Can they claim that this outcome represents something illiberal and unreasonable? They might say that they are being *forced to accept* these interventions as part of contemporary life. How much ethical force should be given to that phrase and that complaint?

In the current debates (2021–22) regarding COVID-19 there is intense discussion about vaccine mandates. Individuals might be denied access to a classroom or to a restaurant or to another country if they have not been vaccinated against Covid-19. That is clearly a restriction on their liberty, though the public health justification for that restriction is quite compelling, given the risks of death associated with infection with that virus. Still, in spite of that rationale, no one is being literally strapped down and sedated so that they can be vaccinated against their will. That would be an instance of liberally unjustified coercion. How does that compare to right to life advocates being *forced to accept* abortion, or physician aid-in-dying or stem cell therapies? What they clearly cannot justifiably say is that their own lives are being altered in any substantive way. No one is demanding that they must be willing to accept any of these procedures for themselves. No one is demanding that they must now be silent in their opposition to these procedures. No one is preventing them from expressing their opposition in various public forums. In short, none of their fundamental rights are threatened.

What religious advocates are prevented from doing, however, is interfering directly in the lives of others to prevent them from obtaining whatever those others see as the benefits of these interventions. Right to life advocates do not have the right to violate the privacy rights or liberty rights of anyone who seek to access these procedures. That is a violation of the fundamental rights of others for no compelling public reason. Right to life advocates might choose to justify their interference in the lives of others by contending that anyone who takes advantage of these interventions is guilty of murder. However, this is hyperbolic rhetoric that has no part in reasonable democratic deliberation. Again, if such rhetoric is given credibility, then extreme advocates for animal rights can denounce as genocide the yearly slaughter of cattle and pigs to satisfy our taste for burgers and hot dogs. They could also expect that right to life advocates would join them in their crusade to prevent the slaughter of innocent animals. So far, no evidence exists of a joining of these political forces.

4.2 Religious Advocates, National Health Insurance, and Choosing Covered Services

What we have emphasized here is the reasonable expectation of noninterference in the lives of others by religious advocates opposed to various ethically controversial medical interventions, so long as those interventions do not violate the rights of others or some legitimate public interest. If that is regarded as being coercive in any sense at all, it is a very innocuous form of coercion. More problematic might be the following situation. Would some form of national health insurance be required by Rawls' notion of political justice? For the sake of argument, I will assume an affirmative answer to this question. I do not believe that argument would have to be very complicated. How just can it be for young adults to be faced with premature death from, say, some form of cancer or heart disease for which we have very expensive but very effective medical interventions which such individuals cannot afford because their employer does not provide health insurance as a benefit? No one of any age should be faced with such a tragic situation; therefore, national health insurance is ethically necessary as a matter of justice.

The harder question pertains to the scope of benefits covered by national health insurance in a liberal pluralistic society. Will national health insurance include coverage for elective abortions, or physician aid-in-dying, or in vitro fertilization and PGD for couples who know they are at risk for having a child with a serious genetic disorder that will very adversely affect both length of life and quality of life, such as cystic fibrosis or some form of hemophilia? I would assume that national health insurance would be paid for through some form of taxation. The obvious problem is that our religious advocates would be deeply ethically conflicted by the fact that they would be paying for these procedures through their taxes when they regarded all these procedures as evil and contrary to the will of God. Taxation, of course, is coercive. How should liberal citizens address this challenge? Should all such ethically controversial medical procedures from some religious perspective be excluded from the benefit package? The expectation would be that anyone needing any of these procedures would have to anticipate the possibility of such a need and purchase some form of private add-on insurance. That would seem to be a very simple solution. However, the real world will readily interfere with the simplicity of that solution.

4.2.1 National Health Insurance and Preimplantation Genetic Diagnosis

Imagine a couple that both know they are carriers of a cystic fibrosis mutation. That means there is a 25 percent chance of their having a child with a cystic fibrosis and a life expectancy of about thirty years. If they were concerned about hemophilia, a son would have a 50 percent chance of having hemophilia. Those risks in both cases could be reduced to zero if they availed themselves of IVF and PGD. However, the cost of achieving a successful pregnancy that way would be about $40,000. Few couples outside the very secure middle class could afford that cost. Should this intervention be part of a national health insurance package, despite the fact that religious advocates would strongly object to the creation of all these excess embryos that would have to be genetically analyzed? There is more complexity here than we might realize at first. We need to ask how any of these couples would know or suspect that they were at risk for having a child with a serious genetic disorder that would adversely affect the length of life or quality of life of that child. Family history might provide some clues but not certainty. Certainty could be achieved with whole genome sequencing (WGS) of both individuals. That would be at a cost of about $5,000. Will that be covered by a national health insurance program? That will raise essentially the same problem for religious advocates since the intent behind this use of WGS would be to make reproductive decisions that were contrary to the ethical commitments of some religious advocates. We should add that yet another option is available, namely, fetal screening with WGS, which can be accomplished noninvasively.[58] The obvious reason for such screening would be to provide the option of abortion if serious genetic deficiencies are identified in the fetus. Would we imagine fetal WGS would be an option for every pregnancy? Should that too be funded through national health insurance?

As noted already, what is wrong with the option of allowing individuals to buy add-on private insurance rather than including ethically controversial medical services in a national health insurance plan? The short answer is that such insurance would be very expensive. The only people who would be motivated to purchase such insurance would be couples who were close to choosing to conceive children. Insurance companies refer to this as the "moral hazard" problem. If my personal physician tells me I likely have a serious treatable cancer, I cannot go out and buy special health insurance that would cover that extraordinary cost. Insurance companies would either refuse to sell me such insurance, or they would price it very close to the expected cost of my cancer treatment. The same applies when a couple plans to have children and has concerns about genetic risks for that child. In practice, what this means is that only upper-middle-class couples would be able to afford either preimplantation genetic diagnosis (PGD) or WGS for either themselves or a fetus. Their children would be born very healthy whereas the children of those below them on the economic scale would be at risk for a broad range of serious genetic disorders that could have been avoided. In the United States that represents about 120,000 babies each year.

If there were nothing we could do about that outcome, we accept it as tragic and regrettable. However, we do have several things that can be done, including WGS, WGS of fetuses, and PGD. All those children will be faced with considerable suffering and premature death. For Rawlsian political liberals preventing that suffering and premature death is what would justify public funding through some form of national health insurance. Advocates for a right to life perspective oppose all these interventions, but they would most oppose being forced to pay taxes to support such programs. One of the practical implications of their own choices will be the birth of children with these various genetic disorders to their coreligionists. These children will certainly not be allowed to simply suffer and die. Instead, they will have enormous costly health care needs as well as costly educational and social service needs, all in an effort to make their lives as satisfactory as possible.

4.2.2 National Health Insurance, Duchenne Muscular Dystrophy, and Cystic Fibrosis

To give a couple of quick illustrations, a patient with Duchenne Muscular Dystrophy DMD) will have initial annual medical costs of $20,000 per year which will rise to $300,000 per year in the later stages of the disease. Roughly 700 DMD patients are born each year in the United States with a life expectancy of twenty years. Cystic fibrosis (CF) patients will have lifetime medical costs of $300,000 to $1 million depending upon mild, moderate, or severe forms. Patients with the more moderate forms can live into their mid-forties or beyond. Life expectancy might improve with a new drug, ivacaftor, which costs $300,000 per year, or $9 million for thirty years of life. Patients with lysosomal storage diseases also need new drugs that cost $300,000 per year.

I mention all these statistics because children with these disorders will certainly be born to right to life advocates who will refrain from using any of the medical interventions discussed in Section 4.2.1. That means that the medical, educational, and social costs associated with the special needs of these children will be paid for through taxes imposed on everyone. Rawlsian political liberals will pay those taxes because they see this as an ethical obligation necessary to provide as decent a life as possible for these children, though they will feel bad that their parents made these choices even though other choices were available to them that would have spared society those costs and suffering. I need to add that even though they might feel badly and wish that these parents would have made different choices, they respect the right of these parents to make these choices as reasonable choices in a liberal society.

4.2.3 Reciprocity, Public Reason, and National Health Insurance

Recall that the most fundamental commitments of a liberal society are to equality and liberty and fair terms of cooperation (or reciprocity). Given these commitments, it would seem fair and reasonable that right to life advocates would be willing to pay taxes to support WGS for reproductive purposes and PGD. Clearly, they are ethically troubled by the choice of these interventions. However, other political liberals are equally troubled by *their choices*, given the suffering that will be endured by those children and their premature deaths. Such an expectation is not unreasonable. Further, the savings achieved would ultimately cover the cost of these procedures with additional savings available to help offset the special needs of the children born to right to life advocates. This last point may be characterized as the "efficiency argument" in support of public funding for PGD. In addition, there is the procreative liberty argument coupled with a public interest argument. Parents who choose PGD to avoid the birth of a child with a serious genetic deficiency are not violating the rights of anyone else, nor is that choice a threat to any public interest. On the contrary, the public interest is the avoidance of predictable harm to future possible children, not to mention the excess social costs needed to care adequately for these children. These are also legitimate concerns of future possible parents who would want to avoid such harms to their children in accord with an ethical commitment to procreative beneficence. All these considerations are clearly within the scope of public reason as opposed to any comprehensive doctrine. This is about reciprocity and fair terms of cooperation.

The conclusion of the prior paragraphs is that it would be just and liberally legitimate to provide public funding for a program that would underwrite the costs of PGD for couples who knew, or had good reason to believe, that they were at risk of having a child with a serious genetic disorder that would very adversely affect the length of life or quality of life of a future possible child. If right to life advocates accepted the argument about fair terms of cooperation in this regard, it would be reasonable for them to expect boundaries on those fair terms. For example, couples might know that they and their future possible children were at risk for serious genetic disorders that would likely emerge late in life, such as Parkinson's or early-onset Alzheimer's or some form of cancer or heart disease with a strong genetic component. It would not be unreasonable to deny public funding for the use of PGD in those circumstances. Efficiency considerations might be the strongest argument to support that view. There would be billions of dollars in costs for PGD for that purpose at the front end, but the hoped-for savings would only be achieved many decades into the future. That would have justice-relevant implications in the present. We have only limited resources (money) to meet virtually unlimited health care needs in the present. How high a priority should this form of preventive PGD have relative to the need to treat all manner of life-threatening medical disorders in the present? Given progress in medical research over a period of decades, interventions might be available for curing or ameliorating many of these genetically related disorders, thereby negating the value of currently costly use of PGD.

4.2.4 Procreative Beneficence and National Health Insurance

Another potential problem should be noted. We mentioned in Section 4.2.3 that many potential parents might see the use of PGD as an ethical commitment, a matter of procreative beneficence. Should there be limits on procreative beneficence? That will strike many as an ethically odd question? However, Julian Savulescu[59] is a strong advocate for a very expansive use of procreative beneficence. He is actually an advocate for the eugenic selection of the best embryo that is likely to yield the best possible life (health-wise) for that future possible child.[60] What this could mean in practice is that hundreds of thousands of future possible parents whose future possible children were not at any identifiable risk for serious health problems would nevertheless choose to pursue PGD rather than normal sexual intercourse in order to have available a dozen or so embryos that could all be genetically analyzed (WGS) so that they could choose that embryo that they believed had the best genetic endowment. Advocates for a right to life position would undoubtedly vigorously object to any public funding for such efforts. They would see millions of excess embryos created and destroyed to satisfy the eugenic whims of potential parents. Consequently, they would oppose any sort of public funding for such parental choices. Note, however, that Rawlsian liberals might not see that reasoning by itself as being compelling. But they would still reject public funding on grounds that no public interest would be served by such funding; it would be a purely personal interest that was being satisfied. In addition, this would be a wasteful and unjust use of public resources. These are clearly public reasons that right to life advocates can endorse just as readily as Rawlsian liberals.

The further question that would need to be addressed would be whether legally banning the use of PGD for this purpose would be liberally legitimate. That is, if these potential parents paid for this procedure entirely from their own resources, what would justify a policy banning such a procedure in these circumstances? Is there a public interest that would be harmed by permitting the practice? Or should this be seen as being within the scope of procreative liberty? How would we imagine this deliberation might go within the context of liberal public reason? I will leave these as open questions.

5 Public Reason: Criticisms from Religious Advocates

To summarize, public reason liberals, such as Rawls, cannot be justifiably accused of coercively denying the rights of reasonable religious advocates to participate in multiple forms of public deliberation regarding ethically controversial medical interventions and technologies. However, as noted earlier, we ought to distinguish informal public deliberation about these matters from more formal public deliberation that is an integral part of a policymaking process. Recall that an integral part of the policymaking process is the need to justify to all who are affected by these policy decisions that these decisions are reasonable and rational. At the very least that requires that the reasons and reasoning intended to justify any policy decision be *accessible or intelligible* to those affected by that policy, even if that policy remains unacceptable to them. That goal is essential to protecting the stability of a liberal, pluralistic society by showing that the proposed policies are legitimate and congruent with the liberal foundations of that society. Expecting that individuals in policymaking roles would function *as citizens expressing their views through public reason* serves to assure stability, as opposed to invoking reasons and reasoning connected to a comprehensive doctrine that could undermine stability. Recall that Rawls is seeking to persuade his reader of the reasonableness of this perspective. Rawls is encouraging civility in these conversations. Rawls sees such civility as a moral obligation, not a legal obligation. Ultimately, it is a hypothetical obligation: If you wish to protect the stable foundations of a liberal, pluralistic society, then you will embrace the role of citizen and the utility of public reason for achieving that goal, and you will encourage your fellow citizens to do the same. Adopting such a role is not something forcefully imposed upon advocates for religious comprehensive views, nor is this something that would undermine the integrity of reasonable religious advocates.

5.1 Is Public Reason Rootless?

Advocates for the inclusion of religious reasons in the formation of public policies related to controversial bioethics issues will offer a number of criticisms of Rawls' conception of public reason. In the remainder of this Element, I want to consider those criticisms and respond to them. Plant[61] contends that public reason is "rootless," and that it needs to be rooted in first-order comprehensive doctrines. Plant contends that the ultimate justification of liberal institutions must be in the primary values of significant moral communities; otherwise, the members of those communities would have no reason to attach themselves to liberal institutions. Plant writes: "Political structures have to grow our of what Hegel called 'the ethical life of a society'; and if the values embodied in such structures are not in fact rooted in that ethical life as it is lived in significant moral communities, then such liberalism will be rootless."[62]

Rawls can readily accept the legitimacy of Plant's criticism, but then add immediately that his conception of liberalism and public reason are very much rooted in our political history since the period of the Enlightenment. In one of his early essays, Rawls calls attention "to an impasse in our recent political history; the course of democratic thought over the past two centuries, say, shows that there is no agreement on the way basic social institutions should be arranged if they are to conform to the freedom and equality of citizens as moral persons."[63] Those notions of freedom and equality are among the most fundamental notions in the public culture of a democratic society. But there have been numerous practical circumstances in which we have struggled to find an appropriate balance between these values because there are different understandings of these two concepts. Rawls' political conception of justice seeks to address this challenge by asking "which traditionally recognized principles of freedom and equality, or which natural variations thereof, would free and equal moral persons agree upon, if they were fairly represented solely as such persons and thought of themselves as citizens living a complete life in an ongoing society?"[64] Rawls adds almost immediately that "we are not trying to find a conception of justice suitable for all societies regardless of their particular social or historical circumstances."[65] He goes on to say that the goal of political philosophy "is to articulate and make explicit those shared notions and principles thought to be already latent in common sense."[66] However, if common sense is too uncertain, then political philosophy should "propose to it certain conceptions and principles congenial to its most essential convictions and historical traditions" (at 306).[67]

I believe these passages make clear that Rawls' conception of liberalism, political justice, and public reason is not rootless. Embedded in these notions is a long and complex political history in which, as a democratic society, we have struggled to construct suitable interpretations of these notions as applied to specific policy challenges, whether civil rights or abortion rights, or a right to physician aid-in-dying, or using embryos in medical research, and so on. In the quoted passages Rawls speaks of notions and principles "latent in common sense." We should think of that as part of public reason. What Rawls is saying is that common (moral and political) sense is something to which all citizens in a democratic society have access, as opposed to comprehensive secular or religious doctrines. What we collectively construct as a democratic society over time and in response to various political and ethical challenges are "considered ethical and political judgments of justice" that are accessible to any reasonable person. In addition, given value pluralism, we learn how we might balance these values in various circumstances. That is, we develop a capacity to use "reflective equilibrium" successfully in the process of democratic deliberation.[68]

5.2 Is Public Reason Entirely Relativistic?

The next objection to public reason from a religious perspective is that it is entirely relativistic. It lacks secure moral foundations. It represents godless secular rationality, and consequently, it is unable to resolve significant moral controversies. Engelhardt, and a number of his followers, are the primary proponents of this point of view. Engelhardt writes: "We are after God. That is, the dominant secular culture is deaf and blind to God's existence. The result is that, in eschewing a God's eye perspective, morality, bioethics, the state, and the meaning of life are all approached as if everything came from nowhere, were going nowhere, and for no enduring and ultimate purpose."[69] Mark Cherry adds that "philosophy is unable to establish any particular bioethics or understanding of morality as canonical; that is, as definitively true and binding."[70] Of course, Rawls' response to this last sentence would be to ask why either politics or morality must be about truth, most especially in a pluralistic world. Instead, the goal of moral and political problem solving is to find practical solutions that are reasonable, given the need to respect all persons as free and equal, and the need for fair terms of cooperation.

Cherry continues: "Without God to secure the moral project, it no longer possesses definitive moral content or unqualified binding significance. Without God, morality is contingent, culturally, and historically conditioned. As a result, it shatters into numerous incommensurable perspectives."[71] The "incommensurable perspectives" that Cherry has in mind are consequentialism, casuistry, deontology, virtue theory, and so on. However, the same can be said of the hundreds of religious perspectives that are out there in the real world. Whose God is supposed to "secure the moral project"? Is that the Christian Trinitarian God, or Yahweh of Judaism, or Allah of Islam? What Rawls would point out is that both the moral theories and the religious belief systems that comprise our society are all comprehensive doctrines, which do interfere with our social capacity for shared public deliberation regarding the more controversial challenges posed by bioethics and emerging medical technologies. Public reason provides a common practical vocabulary for addressing these issues.

Cherry contends that "one needs to know how God experiences the universe; one needs to take a God's eye perspective. God, as Engelhardt recognizes, provides a foundation for morality in being-in-itself."[72] The obvious critical question would be how one accesses the mind of God. Are there individuals who claim to have accomplished this? And what are the rest of us supposed to do when there are multiple individuals who claim to have accessed the mind of God and give conflicting answers regarding some specific moral or political challenge? Qutb would likely see himself accessing the mind of Allah through the Koran while Jerry Falwell would access the mind of God through the Bible. Further, what is it supposed to mean that the foundation of morality is "in being-in-itself"? What does being-in-itself tell me is the most just way to meet the health care needs of everyone when we have only limited resources to meet virtually unlimited health-care needs? In other words, we need to make health-care rationing decisions justly. Should we spend less on marginally beneficial targeted therapies for metastatic cancer in the elderly, or should we spend more on aducanumab to try slowing a bit the progression of Alzheimer's?[73] Having intimate knowledge of being-in-itself does not appear to be especially enlightening in this regard. The same will be true regarding the use of "spare embryos" for medical research or affirming the moral permissibility of IVF and PGD when a couple knows they are at risk of having a child with a serious genetic disorder.

We are finite temporal beings. We are fallible beings. We must confront complex and evolving social and political problems hampered by the burdens of judgment. We are reasonable beings capable of recognizing and honoring fair terms of cooperation. We recognize that there are many good ways of living good lives. We recognize that our moral and political problems and related norms are constantly evolving in response to emerging technologies, changing economic institutions and practices, changing social practices, changing demographics, changing health care systems and health care needs, changing climate conditions, and so on. All these changes require collective responses that are reasonable, fair, and respectful of the equal rights and liberties of all. Public reason provides an accessible resource for all through which those collective responses can be constructed. Being-in-itself remains in itself for all eternity.

5.3 Is Public Reason a Device of Exclusion?

Another criticism of public reason is that it is a device of exclusion responsible for "weeding out those voices that spoke in an unsanctioned idiom and disciplining moral imaginations into a homogenized false pluralism."[74] What Hurlbut is referring to is the use of the authority of science to transform a moral disagreement into an incontrovertible scientific fact. He has a very specific instance in mind when he offers this criticism, namely, the work of the ethics committee of the American Fertility Society in 1986. That committee had to wrestle with the issue of the ethically appropriate use of human embryos in medical research. Initially, that committee asked whether the human embryo was "an individual," and concluded that since twinning was possible until day fourteen after conception, the embryo, prior to that point in time, was a *pre-embryo*. Consequently, the ethics issue was dissolved by being transformed into an indisputable scientific judgment. This is the sort of thing that Hurlbut is objecting to as ethically illicit. Hurlbut writes: "The concept of the pre-embryo encoded a vision of democratic deliberation in which scientific experts step in to ensure that the terms of ethical deliberation comport with the relevant facts."[75] He continues: "On this view, democratic questions of 'What shall we do?' should defer to scientific declarations of what is the case."[76] This is why Hurlbut describes this as an exercise in exclusion "not easily recognized as such."[77] A normative question, ethical or religious, is subtly changed into a matter of scientific fact. "Science is called upon to assume responsibility for forms of complexity, ambiguity, and disagreement that we would rather not have to shoulder as a society, that we would rather have spoken by the faceless authority of the fact than through our own, far less powerful, far less univocal, but far more personal voices."[78] Hurlbut sees public reason as dominated by science and scientific facts, a univocal voice, that obscures the normative disagreements of our ethical and political life.

To begin with, I do not see this as a fair characterization of public reason. Hurlbut puts a lot of argumentative weight on that one example of the pre-embryo. Perhaps there are other examples. Someone might object to science squelching a moral issue by redefining death on the basis of neurologic criteria, so-called brain death, in order to facilitate access to organs for transplantation that were more viable because better perfused. However, we have had that debate, and that debate was both normative and scientific. That was an instance of the use of public reason, as Rawls would use that term. What science could tell us was that in a given patient there was no brain activity, and there was no medical way to restore that activity because of neuronal death. The normative conclusion that emerged from much debate was that a "person" was no longer there, and consequently, we no longer had a "patient" with rights and interests because that patient was entirely beyond treatment of any kind. Being "brain dead" was not like being in a coma, nor was it Locked-In syndrome, nor was it being in a persistent vegetative state. Rawls would certainly endorse the notion that our ethical and political judgments are fact-dependent, which is not the same as saying that scientific facts determine the outcomes of normative debates.

Scientific facts may limit what is normatively reasonable in the way of identifying ethically relevant options. For example, if someone has been in a coma for three years, we could not justifiably conclude they were likely no longer a person, and therefore, they were a candidate for donating their organs. Patients have been in comas for much longer than that and been restored to consciousness. That fact, plus MRI brain scans, would ethically justify refusing to use that patient as a source of transplant organs no matter how many premature deaths might have been prevented. Though Hurlbut describes public reason as a "univocal voice" dominated by science, Rawls repeatedly refers to normative disagreements within public reason that are not going to be resolved by some scientific discovery. Science is about truth. What Rawls emphasizes is that our normative disagreements are practical in character, and the goal of public deliberation is to identify potential resolutions of that disagreement that are reasonable (not true), that represent fair terms of social cooperation. "Political constructivism does not criticize, then, religious, philosophical, or metaphysical accounts of the truth of moral judgments and of their validity. Reasonableness is its standard of correctness, and given its political aims, it need not go beyond that."[79]

5.4 Is Public Reason Incomplete?

The next criticism of public reason is that it is incomplete, inconclusive, inadequate, or hopelessly vague. Defenders of Rawls have had to struggle with responding to this criticism (Quong,[80] LaFont,[81] Miller[82]). Critics have been abundant. DeMarneffe, for example, will contend that "the issue of abortion suggests, then, that there are important liberal positions on the scope of basic liberty that cannot be adequately defended in terms of liberal political values alone."[83] More specifically, he says that if a liberal endorses "the value of human life," then that endorsement is not compatible with permitting abortion for any reason. Quinn elaborates on this point.[84] On the one hand, the equality of women is at stake as a fundamental value. Rawls contends that the equality of women would be severely compromised if fetal life were granted priority. On the other hand, critics of Rawls will contend that respect for human life will have substance and force as a value only if fetal life is given overriding force in this context. Quinn asks how these two fundamental values are supposed to be balanced using only the limited resources of liberal public reason, and he concludes public reason is simply inadequate for addressing such questions (which would seem to include many of the more controversial issues in bioethics). Eberle and Cuneo will contend that public reason is not "rich enough to provide compelling reasons to support genuinely informative positions on matters of basic justice or constitutional essentials."[85] Quinn echoes this same point, then adds that "since public reason denies itself the resources of all comprehensive doctrines, it is not obvious that it has enough content to yield such answers in almost all cases. It must be applied to hard cases to determine whether it yields reasonable public answers."[86] Quinn contends that both common sense and science are befuddled by the abortion issue. They are unable to offer anything helpful by way of addressing the conflict of values. Quinn then concludes that two options are open to the defender of liberal public reason. The first is to say that there are two reasonable balances "because its resources are too weak to single out just one reasonable balance."[87] The other is to say that there is no reasonable balance "because its resources are too weak to determine any reasonable balance."[88]

Quinn sees this indeterminacy as happening repeatedly in the contemporary world. It would be a serious understatement to say an outcome such as this is unacceptable. The introduction of contentious medical practices requires some sort of determinate and legitimate social response. If public reason is "too weak" to yield that response, then something more is needed. Kent Greenawalt argues that "when people reasonably think that shared premises of justice and criteria for determining truth cannot resolve critical questions of fact, fundamental questions of value, or the weighing of competing benefits and harms, they do appropriately rely on religious convictions that help them answer these questions."[89] This is actually a conclusion that Rawls can endorse and that does not diminish the utility or legitimacy of liberal public reason.

The generic Rawlsian solution would be to say that as a social policy we will respect the equal liberty of all. Thus, individuals who are religiously opposed to abortions will refrain from seeking an abortion and will endorse that restriction through their religious community. Likewise, if they are opposed to physician aid-in-dying, they will refrain from seeking that service, no matter how painful the end stages of their life might be, again with the support of their religious community. Further, if they are faced with difficulties in conceiving a child through normal sexual intercourse, they will refrain from seeking IVF and creating excess embryos. The same will be true if they have concerns about the conception of a child who will be afflicted with a genetic disorder that might result in premature death or unnecessary suffering. Further, they should see themselves, as liberal citizens committed to equal respect for the rights of their fellow citizens, as supportive of the rights of their fellow citizens to choose for themselves any of the above medical interventions, given that none of these interventions represent a threat to the rights of others or to clear public interests. This is not the end of public discussion regarding any of these matters. Citizens on both sides of the divide in these cases may still recognize the need for various regulations that would govern any of the above practices for, among other things, protecting the safety of these patients and preventing their being exploited in various ways. These would be matters for public deliberation using the resources of liberal public reason. For the sake of clarity, we will work out below an example of what that deliberation might look like with regard to a future possible artificial womb. Before turning to that task, we need to explore a bit more carefully a Rawlsian response to the criticism that public reason is inadequate, indeterminate, incomplete, and so on.

5.5 Public Reason is Complete

We may start with a passage from Rawls in which he explicitly asserts that public reason is complete. Rawls writes:

> "We want the substantive content and the guidelines of inquiry of a political conception, when taken together, to be complete. That means that the values specified by that conception can be suitably balanced or combined, or otherwise united, as the case may be, so that those values alone give a reasonable public answer to all, or to nearly all, questions involving the constitutional essentials and basic questions of justice."[90]

This passage requires some careful interpretation. Rawls' critics contend that public reason is inadequate and incomplete. As noted, they can cite any number of contemporary controversies discussed by bioethicists that do not seem to have a satisfactory resolution without bringing in material from various comprehensive doctrines.

Perhaps we can start by saying that I am certain Rawls does not believe that public reason is "complete" in the way that mathematical reason might be complete. In other words, in the world of mathematics we have axioms and all manner of rules and formulas, and principles of operation logically connected in such a way that any mathematical problem can be solved with religious attention to the correct application of those rules. All the answers to all mathematical problems are embedded in that system, which makes it complete.[91] A computer could just crank out all those answers without any need for public deliberation. For Rawls, however, public reason will necessarily require public deliberation. Why would there need to be concern about the "burdens of judgment" if that were not the case? However, that suggests incompleteness.

Where is the completeness that Rawls has in mind? Perhaps we should think about it this way. At the most fundamental level of political justice, we find the notions of equal rights and equal political liberties for all persons, along with a commitment to seeking fair terms of cooperation and a recognition of a plurality of reasonable political values. These are then the broad notions that must guide the construction and legitimation of the constitutional essentials, which include fundamental political rights "and fundamental principles that specify the general structure of government and the political process, the powers of the legislature, executive and the judiciary; the scope of majority rule . . . ."[92] What needs to be noticed is that there are many types of democratic governments that would satisfy the requirements of Rawls' conception of political justice and liberal public reason. The structure of the US government is (essentially) just as legitimate from the perspective of political justice and liberal public reason as the government of Germany or Great Britain.[93] It is unlikely that the same could be said of the current structure of government in either the Russian Federation or China. Is it the case that we have in the US Constitution a complete specification of all the most fundamental political rights guaranteed to every citizen? I will hypothesize that something might be missing. However, that would not imply that liberal public reason was incomplete. We would have to consider some future possible proposed fundamental rights that might or might not be congruent with those most fundamental features of our conception of political justice and liberal public reason. The point is that the intellectual resources are there to make those judgments. In that sense, Rawls can say that public reason is complete.

There is another sense in which public reason might be judged to be incomplete. As Rawls notes, "public reason often allows more than one reasonable answer to any particular question."[94] This is because there are many reasonable political values and many ways in which they might be interpreted in their application to specific circumstances. Rawls acknowledges that this will be especially true when we must create policies for addressing social and economic inequalities. He writes: "These matters are nearly always open to wide differences of reasonable opinion; they rest on complicated inferences and intuitive judgments that require us to assess complex social and economic information about topics poorly understood."[95]

Imagine, for example, that we wanted to put in place some form of national health insurance for everyone in the United States. How should we determine the scope of health-care services that will be covered and health-care needs that will be met? We might imagine that the simplest answer would be to cover the entire population with Medicare. After all, Medicare has been around for more than fifty years and seems to be widely accepted. However, portions of the Medicare program have 20 percent co-pay requirements. Consequently, many of the elderly purchase private supplementary insurance to cover those co-pays. In the case of what are called Tier IV prescription drugs, which tend to be extraordinarily expensive, the co-pay could be 30 percent or more. Individuals who cannot cover that co-pay will be denied those drugs and the health benefits they promise. Americans in the upper half of the income spectrum will be able to purchase that supplementary private insurance. That will largely not be true for Americans in the lower half of the income spectrum. Is that something that would need to be "fixed" somehow as a matter of political justice? Should those co-pays be abolished for everyone so that there are no financial barriers to needed drugs?

Health policy analysts will argue that the point of the co-pays was to make patients think more carefully about whether a particular drug was "worth it" to them because they would need to make a substantial investment. Among the drugs where these issues would be raised most painfully would be the "targeted" cancer therapies for patients with metastatic disease.[96] Virtually all these drugs have a cost of $100,000–$150,000 per year or for a course of treatment. None of them are curative. For most patients, the gains in life expectancy are measurable in months, not years, though there are the patients called "super responders" who might gain extra years of life. These patients represent just a tiny fraction of metastatic cancer patients.[97] No one knows why they have such a dramatic response. Nor do we have the ability to identify such patients before the fact using some medical test. How are such patients supposed to determine whether they should use most of their retirement savings in the hope they might be among the 2 percent of patients who are super responders? We can save patients that mental agony by agreeing to pay the full costs of these drugs with public funds, though we obviously have to consider whether this is a good use of public resources when the cost is so high, the likelihood of substantial benefit so low, and multiple other health care priorities needing funding.

What I have written here represents only a tiny fraction of the complexity associated with trying to create some form of national health insurance in the United States. We have only limited resources (money) for meeting virtually unlimited health care needs. An enormous number of reasonable possible trade-offs and balancing options are available, with respect to which public reason can offer no answer that represents the "most just" choice possible, though public reason can exclude some options that were either unjust or "not just enough." This is not a flaw of public reason but an ineliminable feature of the complexity of our health care world and its financing. This does not mean public reason is inadequate. What it means is that public reason must be supplemented by and evolve through fair and inclusive processes of public deliberation. This is a point emphasized by Cristina Lafont. She writes: "Consequently, and contrary to Wolterstorff's contention, democratic citizens cannot determine in advance of actual public deliberation the reasons upon which their political decisions ought to be based. In order to be legitimate, their decisions ought to be based on those reasons that have survived the scrutiny of public deliberation in the public sphere."[98] In other words, public deliberation is integral to public reason in a liberal democratic society, unlike the situation with some comprehensive religious doctrines where the answer to any of these questions is available before the fact from either scripture or some religious authority.

6 Democratic Deliberation and the Evolution of Public Reason

The other point that is implicit in this last paragraph, and that we called attention to earlier, is that public reason becomes ethically and politically richer, more reliable, and more legitimate through addressing specific complex cases such as have been emerging in medicine and bioethics. Quong[99] emphasizes this point as well as Jeremy Williams (2015). Williams writes in this regard that if Rawlsian public reason liberals "are to make their case more conclusively in the future, both those who affirm and those who dispute public reason's power to resolve complex moral problems will have to engage in a close case-by-case analysis of particular issues, isolating the public reasons relevant to them, and evaluating how much work these can do in enabling citizens to draw appropriate conclusions" (2015, at 26). We turn then to a specific illustration of this point, using the case of the artificial womb.

6.1 The Artificial Womb: Is There a Need?

Let's start by stating that the artificial womb case I will be discussing is purely hypothetical at this point. Research on such a technology has been ongoing for at least thirty years. There have been promises of a working model "very soon" all along the way. The likely reality is that it could be created in the next ten to thirty years. To be clear, we are referring to a technology that would make possible the gestation of a fetus from conception until birth nine months later. The obvious initial question is why would we need such a technology? Is this just a technical medical challenge? The short answer to both questions is that there is a need of sorts. That need would be the situation of women who did not have a uterus capable of carrying a pregnancy for any length of time at all. As things are now, an option for some women would be the use of a surrogate who would serve as the gestational host for an embryo conceived by the couple and implanted in the surrogate. There are only twelve US states that legally permit surrogacy (Hatch Egg Donation & Surrogacy, 2022). Further, there have been situations where a surrogate mother became attached to the baby and refused to surrender the baby at birth. The Baby M was the first such instance (Haberman, 2014). It generated considerable legal and ethical controversy. Other problems pertain to the trustworthiness of the surrogate mother with regard to diet during the pregnancy, as well as refraining from smoking, alcohol, and unapproved drugs, or engaging in any behavior that might endanger the pregnancy. Further, the expectation was that a surrogate mother would agree to an abortion if serious fetal anomalies were discovered during the pregnancy. Virtually all of these issues would be irrelevant if an artificial womb were available for the entirety of the pregnancy.

6.2 Should We Permit Research to Create an Artificial Womb?

Our key question would be this: What sort of public policy issues might arise in connection with research regarding an artificial womb and its eventual implementation in the clinical world as a birth option? We can start with the question of whether a liberal pluralistic society could forbid the actual development of this technology. It is easy enough to imagine objections that would quickly emerge from more conservative religious perspectives. If something as simple as contraception is rejected as unnatural, an unethical interruption of the reproductive process designed by God, then certainly the artificial womb will be seen as being even more unnatural.

Older readers will recall the debates in the early 1970s regarding IVF, before Louise Brown was born, the first child to be conceived in vitro in 1978. Edwards and Steptoe were the researchers who had spent many years developing the capacity for IVF. The predictions from many critics of their work were that children who were conceived outside the womb would end up being deformed in multiple sorts of ways.[100] Of course, none of these predictions came true. In the United States today, more than 75,000 children are born each year who are IVF babies. Some of these children are born with genetic or developmental deformities, but those numbers are no greater than in the case of a normal birth. Still, the complexity associated with maintaining an entire pregnancy ex utero is many times greater than anything with IVF (or any of its reproductive variants).

What I will assume for the sake of discussion is that the artificial womb researchers would have gestated some mammal from conception to birth as a proof of concept. However, that would hardly allow us to conclude that such a successful experiment would assure comparable success with the first human effort. It would not be unreasonable to expect some number of initial failures. How should those be thought about before the fact from a moral and political perspective? Keep in mind that the artificial womb would be entirely transparent for the entire pregnancy, unlike a normal pregnancy that is mostly hidden from prying medical eyes. In other words, if it was evident that something very serious was going wrong, the experiment (the fetus) would be aborted. On the one hand, we could imagine this outcome being "excused" as the sort of thing that can happen in a normal pregnancy that would result in a mother choosing to have an abortion. On the other hand, the reasonable suspicion would be that something went wrong, not because of some biological flaw, but because of a design flaw in the artificial womb itself. Would that put that outcome in a different moral or political category? Or would this be no different than bad things that can happen with experimental medicine in the case of children with life-threatening illnesses who would have no other option? In other words, the outcome would be tragic and unfortunate but not something ethically blame-worthy. Or is this research intrinsically unethical, as Leon Kass has contended?[101] Note that I am not trying to offer any conclusive moral or political judgments in this regard. I am presenting the elements of public reason that might come into play during a public conversation regarding the issue of permitting this research.

6.3 The Value of the Artificial Womb

I want to take this analysis one step further. Assume the research is successful. The artificial womb is safe and effective. In fact, we could imagine that it was safer and more effective in delivering a normal baby than natural pregnancy. This is not hard to imagine. A woman carrying a normal pregnancy can be exposed to a considerable array of toxic substances in the environment with respect to which she was entirely ignorant through no fault of her own. In some cases, the result would be the loss of the pregnancy. In other cases, the developmental damage might not manifest itself until the first few years of life. That damage was not preventable, nor might it be reparable. These sorts of tragic outcomes would be obviated through the use of the artificial womb. Moreover, various medical issues can arise for the fetus that today are treatable, though actual treatment is risky to both the fetus and the mother because access to the fetus would be through the mother. One such example would be spina bifida, the adverse consequences of which can be dramatically reduced if surgery is performed in the womb to correct that problem (the hydrocephalus and exposed spinal cord). Again, a key virtue of the artificial womb is that it is transparent, and the fetus is accessible.

We must also note that pregnancy and delivery can pose a considerable number of risks to the mother. There are the discomforts of backache and nausea associated with pregnancy. But there are also much more serious risks. One research study found that as many as 60,000 women each year in the United States were affected by severe maternal morbidity, "unexpected outcomes of labor or delivery that had serious short- or long-term impacts."[102] A short list of the relevant morbidities would include blood loss, disseminated intravascular coagulation, sepsis, shock, pulmonary edema, acute heart failure, eclampsia, adult respiratory distress syndrome, and so on. At the end of the list would be the 700 women who die each year in the US in connection with childbirth. We should also call attention to mental health issues, such as post-partum depres-sion, which includes the risk of suicide. A social/ political/ economic argument might also be made for wide accessibility to the artificial womb, namely, the loss of job opportunities and promotions as a consequence of either the pregnancy itself or potential related morbidities. Anna Smajdor[103] has contended that access to the artificial womb should be thought of as a moral imperative for our society, a matter of justice. The goal would be to minimize the harms related to pregnancy, which certainly seems like a legitimate public interest, and the protection of fair equality of women for various social and economic benefits.[104] Her arguments have precipitated quite a debate, but I wish to put that aside for the moment.

6.4 The Artificial Womb and Procreative Liberty

Having called attention to all the health risks, inconveniences, and loss of financial opportunities associated with a natural pregnancy, what would justify from a liberal perspective restricting this technology to women who were incapable of gestating a fetus and giving birth in the normal way. The artificial womb would seem to offer numerous advantages to both that future possible child and to the potential mother. Those advantages would seem to be ethically substantive, which is to say that a woman seeking to have a child could not rightly be accused of wanting to access the artificial womb on the basis of a whim. In other words, this looks like a reasonable use of procreative liberty. In addition, no obvious public interest would seem to speak against any couple seeking to use this technology to have a baby. In other words, a liberal society would have to be fairly permissive in this regard. That would include single mothers, gay couples, and lesbian couples who wished to have a child in this way. I will mention one regulation that would appear to be legally necessary. Both members of a couple would have to agree to the use of this technology. A husband would not have the legal right to demand that his wife have a natural pregnancy because that was the way he was born, or that was what his family would expect.

6.5 Abortion Permissibility and the Artificial Womb

The most ethically and politically challenging issue associated with the artificial womb would be abortion. Most of my readers will recall the classic abortion article by Judith Jarvis Thomson, "A Defense of Abortion."[105] In that article she imagines The Society of Music Lovers spiriting her away in the middle of the night and hooking her up to a world-famous violinist who needs her kidneys for a limited period of time to survive. Thomson awakes in the morning to find this stranger attached to her. After hearing the circumstances of his attachment, she demands her physicians detach him. She has not given permission for this individual to use her body. It does not matter that he needs her body for life itself. The violinist, of course, represents a fetus that has come to occupy her body against her will (and there are numerous ways in which a pregnancy can be nonvoluntary). The critical comment Thomson makes in this essay occurs when the violinist is detached. If he miraculously survives the detachment, Thomson states explicitly that she would have no right to kill him. This has obvious implications with respect to the artificial womb.

First, there are no nonvoluntary pregnancies with the artificial womb. A couple has made that deliberate choice. Second, a woman cannot claim that the fetus no longer has the right to use her body, that she is withdrawing the permission she may have given originally, or perhaps because her husband abandoned her four months into the pregnancy. The fetus is safely in the artificial womb. Third, the life and health of the mother are not a risk because the fetus is not connected to her. Fourth, she might have second thoughts about being a mother, or the quality of her marriage, of her changed financial circumstances. She cannot simply say that she wants the fetus removed from the artificial womb at four months and allow it to die, asserting at the same time that she had a legal right to an abortion. What she is really demanding is the death of the fetus when the fetus is perfectly safe in the artificial womb. It seems this is precisely what Thomson said she had no right to demand.

This last point can be more readily appreciated if we think about current practice in Neonatal Intensive Care Units (NICUs) regarding very premature infants. An infant born at twenty-two or twenty-three weeks has a very poor prognosis, both with regard to bare survival and with regard to survival with impairments that will reduce considerably both length of life and quality of life. At that point parents are given the option of comfort care only, or an aggressive effort to save the infant's life. Parents might choose aggressive care, but a couple weeks later the infant experiences a Grade IV brain bleed that might prove fatal or that might have devastating quality of life effects. The parents would have the moral and legal right to withdraw life-sustaining care at that point. However, if that infant seemed to be doing very well at twenty-eight or twenty-nine weeks, still connected to life-sustaining care, but the parents decided there were still some risks and they might be better off withdrawing care and letting the infant die, they would no longer have that option as an ethical option. Removing the fetus from the artificial womb at three months or four months would seem to be closer to this last scenario than the prior scenario. In the *Roe* v. *Wade* US Supreme Court decision, significant weight seemed to be given to whether the fetus was viable outside the womb. That was in 1973 when very few NICUs existed, and their capacity to save infants below twenty-six weeks was virtually nonexistent. The artificial womb can be seen as the ultimate evolution of the NICU.

Given all this background, our ultimate question is: What sort of policy changes are necessary or permissible with regard to the status of the fetus in the artificial womb or the rights of the parents to choose an abortion in the context of a liberal, pluralistic society committed to addressing such issues through public reason? Can we just say: "Nothing has really changed; parents still have the right to choose abortion for whatever the range of reasons and circumstances where it is currently legally permissible." Note that this statement itself captures a very specific change. In the case of the artificial womb, both parents would have to approve removal of a fetus from the artificial womb. As things are now, the woman alone has the right to make that decision because it is her body. The father of that fetus does not have the right to commandeer her body to satisfy whatever his wishes might be. If the fetus is in an artificial womb both parents would have to agree to any decisions made regarding the fetus, including medical decisions that would otherwise have been carried out in utero. The other change that is obvious is that it is a third party that is caring for that fetus, likely in a hospital setting at considerable distance from the parents. After all, that is the point of the artificial womb. Physicians and other health professionals would be constantly monitoring the health status of the fetus, and they would be prepared to intervene quickly if some adverse health state seemed to be developing. This would often be without any explicit permission from the parents, especially if time did not permit such consultation. That makes the fetus look much more like a patient in the NICU than a fetus inside its mother making occasional trips to the physician's office. Part of what I am beginning to explore here is how a liberal citizen's judgment using public reason regarding the legal permissibility of abortion might be affected by full gestation in an artificial womb. What I will also assume is that nothing would change regarding current abortion rights and the justification for those rights in the case of a natural pregnancy.

We can consider some possible scenarios. We can start by imagining significantly more restrictive policies regarding abortion in the case of the artificial womb. These restrictions would be made very clear to a couple through a stringent process of informed consent at the time the couple was considering the artificial womb. They might be told that for the first six weeks they would have the right to discontinue the pregnancy for any reason at all. After that, if there were serious anomalies in the fetus predictive of very premature death or very compromised quality of life, they would have the right to remove the fetus from the artificial womb.[106] However, a range of personal circumstances would not yield sufficient justification for removing the fetus from the artificial womb beyond those first six weeks. The couple might be in the process of divorcing, or their financial circumstances might have changed dramatically, or one of them might be faced with a serious illness that might prove to be a terminal illness. None of these reasons would represent sufficient justification for removing the fetus from the artificial womb. They would have the right to refuse to raise the child, in which case they would put the child up for adoption, maybe even prior to birth.

Our question is this: Could these restrictions be approved as a matter of liberal public reason and public policy? Would these restrictions not violate any basic rights, such as rights to privacy or procreative liberty? Is there some public interest that is protected by these restrictive considerations? Alternatively, should there be little in the way of public policy with respect to decisions couples make regarding ending pregnancies initiated in the artificial womb? That is, should public policy permit each hospital or health care institution providing access to artificial wombs to have their own rules regarding the circumstances in which a couple could choose to remove a fetus from the artificial womb? Religious institutions could simply forego making available this service if this was contrary to their religious beliefs.

I am not suggesting that a liberal, pluralistic society using the resources of Rawlsian public reason would find an easy or obvious policy solution to these challenges. A pregnancy that is entirely outside a woman's body from conception to birth is a radically different situation from a pregnancy entirely within a woman's body. It at least seems that way, as my comparison to a NICU is intended to suggest. Rasanen wants to argue that even with the existence of the artificial womb parents have a right to the death of the fetus.[107] He offers three arguments in support of that claim: (1) a procreative liberty right, that is, the right not to become a biological parent; (2) a right to genetic privacy; and (3) a right to property. Rasanen tends not to distinguish clearly two very different circumstances, namely, full gestation in the artificial womb as opposed to partial gestation. The latter scenario occurs when a woman chooses to discontinue a pregnancy relatively early on, say, at three months and the artificial womb is out there to "save" the fetus she would otherwise choose to abort. We assume the choice is for social reasons as opposed to medical reasons regarding either the mother or the fetus.

Is refusing the transfer of the fetus to the artificial womb ethically equivalent to Thomson killing the violinist who was successfully detached from her? Rasanen would give a negative answer to this question for the three suggested reasons above. His views have been significantly criticized by a number of bioethicists (Mathison and Davis,[108] Blackshaw and Rodger,[109] Kaczor,[110] Hendricks[111]). Probably the least persuasive argument offered by Rasanen is the property argument. Rasanen calls attention to legal arguments made in American courts regarding the disposition of frozen eight-cell embryos when the parents are divorcing and disagreeing regarding that disposition. Courts treat the status of those embryos *as if* they were property, which is not the same as saying that they are property. This language seems especially inappropriate when a fetus has been entirely gestated in an artificial womb, which seems to make the fetus more like a patient in the care of health care professionals with parents expected to make decisions in the best interest of the fetus, as opposed to their personal interests.[112] However, Kendal will contend, at least in the partial gestation case, that if the woman chooses to transfer the fetus to the artificial womb, this should be regarded as an altruistic act, something she is not ethically obligated to do.[113] That is, she would be behaving as the proverbial Good Samaritan in the Gospels caring for a stranger, as opposed to being the mother of that fetus. We can imagine that this would be another focal point for critical discussion through liberal public reason. However, this rationale does not seem to be relevant in the case of full gestation in the artificial womb, should a woman choose to discontinue that pregnancy at four months.

Privacy considerations would not seem to justify the removal of the fetus from the artificial womb at four months. The fetus is in public space and is the responsibility of the caregivers as well as the parents. It might be argued that parents have the right to make medical decisions for their children. Consider a four-year-old with a terminal cancer. The oncologists want to try a radical experimental treatment, but the parents refuse and remove their child from the hospital. They clearly have that right as responsible parents in that situation. However, if that child had a curable cancer and parents wanted to refuse a very effective treatment, preferring to use a faith healer instead, the hospital could justifiably seek guardianship in order to protect the best interests of that child. Removing a fetus at four months from the artificial womb looks closer to this latter situation, except, of course, the fetus is not a person, though the fetus is clearly moving in that direction. The fetus is also not an embryo, which may be treated as if it were property of the parents. But the fetus cannot be justifiably described as parental property.

Should we say, from the perspective of public reason, that parents have responsibility for the well-being of the fetus in the artificial womb as if it were a premature infant in the NICU?[114] It is easy for me to imagine that fair-minded citizens acting as liberal citizens, free from any commitment to any comprehensive doctrine, religious or not, would struggle with this question. What precisely is it that would give parents in these circumstances a right to the death of the fetus? I would be certain of one intuition, namely, that as a matter of procreative liberty any couple would have the right to consider the artificial womb for the gestation of their pregnancy. A fundamental commitment to liberalism would require that. Perhaps a stringent process of informed consent would be required after that. That process would include an understanding that they could change their mind within the first six or eight weeks after conception. Beyond that, termination of gestation would only be permissible when that was in the best medical interests of the fetus, that is, severe abnormalities. They would have the option of surrendering the fetus/ baby for adoption. This strikes me as a reasonable compromise. However, I can imagine lots of other possibilities that might need to be considered through public reason and a fair process of democratic deliberation. That is the ultimate point Rawls would endorse when he asserts that public reason evolves through the consideration of challenges such as that of the artificial womb.

7 Conclusion

The question we raised at the beginning of this Element was whether religious arguments could provide a reasonable, justified basis for restrictive (coercive) public policies with respect to a broad range of innovative, albeit ethically and politically controversial, medical interventions and technologies, such as research with human embryos, PGD, or the use of artificial wombs. With Rawls, we would give a negative answer to this question. A positive answer would not be congruent with the fundamental values of a liberal, pluralistic society committed to equal concern and respect for all. A positive answer would necessarily involve coercively imposing restrictive policies justified by religious reasons that would not be accessible or acceptable to those who did not share that religious perspective.

Rawls advocates for policies that would address these controversial technologies on the basis of public reasons that were accessible to all, even if not fully agreeable by all. All are invited to be part of the public democratic deliberations that would construct these policies, though all are invited to participate in these deliberations *as citizens* who are agnostic with respect to the truth of all comprehensive doctrines, whether secular or religious. The common language for these deliberations is public reason, which is essentially rooted in common-sense experience and the most reliable science of the day. The goal of public reason and these deliberations is practical, namely, to identify reasonable policy options that reflect fair terms of cooperation in a liberal, pluralistic society and that are stable. Novel medical interventions are presumptively acceptable so long as they do not violate any basic rights or undermine any public interests. These interventions are not imposed upon any religious advocates because they are always free to avoid taking advantage of any of these interventions. In that regard, a Rawlsian liberal society is respecting the integrity of these religious advocates. Further, religious advocates are not treated as second-class citizens because they have the capacity to participate in formal policymaking processes as reasonable liberal citizens and in more informal policy discussions with their full religious commitments. Finally, public reason is not fixed and final; it evolves through the deliberative process and all the novel, emerging social, political, economic, and technological challenges medicine generates for bioethics and related public policies.

A Provocative Postscript

The United States Supreme Court rendered its decision in the case of *Dobbs* v. *Jackson Women's Health Organization* on June 23, 2022. As anticipated, it overturned *Roe* v. *Wade*. Justice Alito wrote the majority opinion. His basic contentions were that (1) "the Constitution makes no express reference to a right to obtain an abortion," nor (2) is the right to obtain an abortion "rooted in the Nation's history and tradition," nor (3) is having access to abortion "an essential component of 'ordered liberty,'" nor (4) does an alleged privacy right or liberty right ground access to abortion as a fundamental right, nor (5) does the doctrine of *stare decisis* speak against overturning *Roe*. Alito concludes that *Roe* was "egregiously wrong and on a collision course with the Constitution from the day it was decided." Alito adds, "The [*Roe*] Court short-circuited the democratic process by closing it to the large number of Americans who disagreed with *Roe*."[1]

This postscript must be brief. A comprehensive critical assessment of the *Dobbs* decision is not possible. However, Rawls has held up as a model of public reason the US Supreme Court.[2] To what extent is that true in the case of *Dobbs*? I will argue that the court is justifiably criticized in a number of respects from the perspective of public reason. We begin with this Court's rejection of *stare decisis*, respect for precedent, with regard to *Roe*. Precedents can be flawed for many sorts of reasons, even major precedents. The Alito opinion cites *Brown* v. *Board of Education* as a decision that justifiably overturned prior decisions that permitted the "separate but equal" doctrine that legitimated racial segregation in education. States that endorsed the "separate but equal" doctrine were violating the fundamental rights of nonwhite students. This was not a matter that could justly be left to the discretionary political authority of state legislative bodies.

Earlier this same week that same court decided a gun control case brought from New York state. In that case the Supreme Court overruled a New York state law that significantly regulated gun possession in public. The Supreme Court judged that those regulations violated Second Amendment rights "to keep and bear arms," in effect saying that the states did not have the right to regulate gun possession in the interest of public safety, despite the gun violence that has captured headlines across the country.[3] By way of contrast, the *Dobbs* opinion denied any constitutionally protected fundamental reproductive rights and left to the states the right to decide to be as restrictive or as liberal as they wished with regard to abortion. The emerging predictable result is chaos and confusion, as well as irrationality and arbitrariness. These are the very characteristics Alito claimed were inherent features of the *Roe* and *Casey* decisions.

Alito noted that the *Roe* decision appealed to a liberty right to justify a woman choosing to have an abortion. However, Alito claimed a simple appeal to a liberty right was much too broad to be constitutionally justified. Such an unregulated right would permit anyone to consume any drug they wished or to party drunk and naked in the streets. Alito contended instead that constitutionally protected liberty had to be "ordered liberty." If women were allowed to have an abortion for any reason at all at any point in a pregnancy, that would be "disordered liberty." Ordered liberty required a balancing of interests, the interests of a woman against the interests of an "unborn human being."[4] Alito claimed that there was no such balancing of interests by *Roe*.[5] Instead, the "unborn human being" was given no weight at all; only the interests of the woman counted.

Alito seems to believe, either naively or perversely, that the individual states will restore an appropriate balance between those competing interests, as required by ordered liberty. However, in at least twenty-six states, the announced intention is to shift the balancing of interests almost entirely in the direction of the "unborn human being." Such a shift would not be unreasonable in the case of a perfectly healthy fetus late in the eighth month that represented no threat to the life or health of its mother. It is much harder (completely unreasonable) to endorse this same conclusion if we compare the "interests" of an eight-cell embryo, or a 200-cell embryo, or a four-week-old fetus to the interests of the mother. The interests of the mother would include all of her normal life responsibilities and challenges, such as earning a living or caring for other children, as well as the risks to her pregnancy-related health, such as gestational diabetes, preeclampsia, gestational hypertension, and so on. These interests are real and substantial. What are supposed to be the comparable interests of an embryo or fetus at less than ten weeks after conception? If we assign unlimited weight to the potential life of an embryo or early fetus, then this is not ordered liberty. This is ordered ideology. This is not congruent with public reason, which must be indifferent to the truth claims of any comprehensive doctrine.[6]

Alito's opinion has not, in actual practice, yielded anything resembling "ordered liberty." Instead, what we see beginning to emerge is legal, medical, social, and ethical chaos. States that have, or are in the process of implementing, the most stringent abortion laws, allowing abortion only in those cases where the mother's life is imminently at risk, are also seeking to find ways to prevent individuals from leaving the state to seek abortions elsewhere.[7] This would seem completely unreasonable unless one attributes virtually infinite weight to protecting the life of that fetus. Additional laws are being proposed that would criminalize speech by physicians, other health professionals, friends, and so on if that speech is aimed at facilitating access to abortion services, such as access to a medical abortion. Is this congruent with First Amendment rights of free speech? Or does the infinite weight accorded to protecting the life of any fetus outweigh rights of free speech in this case? This is only the beginning of legal and medical chaos. It would appear that the court is permitting the states to make the life of the embryo/ fetus a supreme value, contrary to the value pluralism that is integral to public reason and the proper functioning of a liberal democratic society.

Alito goes on to say, "Moreover, we are aware of no common-law case or authority.... that remotely suggests a positive *right* to procure an abortion at any stage of a pregnancy."[8] Again, Alito sees as a major flaw in *Roe* its failure to justify its holding on the basis of history and tradition. Instead, Alito notes that in virtually all states abortion had been outlawed from the middle of the nineteenth century until the middle of the twentieth century. *That* is the precedent that should not have been overturned according to Alito. In addition, no explicit right to an abortion is mentioned in the Constitution. What Alito does not say, but what Judge Clarence Thomas does say, is that the right to contraception was also outlawed in many states for decades, until the *Griswold* decision in 1965 that contended a right to privacy in the "penumbra" of the Constitution assured such a right. Still, if we follow Alito, contraception is never mentioned in the Constitution. Again, if we wish the state to ascribe almost infinite weight to "potential human life," then contraception may be sacrificed as the lesser good. However, such a conclusion would be illiberal and unreasonable, that is, contrary to public reason.

Finally, Alito contends that *Roe* was all wrong because it "short-circuited the democratic process."[9] He seems to believe that overruling *Roe* will reinvigorate democratic debate regarding appropriate limits for seeking an abortion. However, that has already proven to be a false hope (assuming Alito actually entertained such a hope). Alito seemed to suggest in his historical meanderings that more than a hundred years' worth of laws outlawing abortion represented a more legitimate precedent than that of *Roe*. This has resulted in the resurrection of all these laws from a hundred years ago, what are referred to as "zombie" laws. When the *Roe* decision was handed down, all those laws that outlawed abortion became invalid. Though invalid, they remained on the books. This pertains to the US "separation of powers" doctrine. Courts can invalidate a law, but only a legislative body can remove a law from the books. What is wrong with this state of affairs? These "zombie" laws short-circuit democratic debate in the present. They permit the avoidance of political accountability by legislators in the present.

All the legislators responsible for enacting those "zombie" laws are dead, which is to say that there is no current political accountability for the effects of those laws in the present. There is no taking account of all the changes in reproductive medical technology and medical practice that have occurred in the intervening hundred years since these laws were passed, such as our capacity to provide infertile couples with access to in vitro fertilization so that they can have children or preimplantation genetic diagnosis to identify embryos with life-threatening genetic disorders. Likewise, there is no taking account of cultural changes during those hundred years, most especially attention to protecting the equal rights of women in multiple areas of our social, political, and economic life.

Allowing these "zombie laws" to be resurrected is a perfect example of an unaccountable dead hand from the past governing our medical and political life today. Current legislators, mindful of all the controversy around the abortion issue, can duck their democratic responsibility to thoughtfully consider with their constituents what sort of regulation of abortion is most appropriate and reasonable in a liberal, pluralistic, tolerant democratic society. This is ethically and politically wrong. This is a failure to engage public reason and to formulate reasonable public policies. In brief, it is cowardly.

Responsible legislators should be willing to engage in the ethically and medically complex, difficult public conversations necessary to forge reasonable policies regarding abortion in any state seeking to allow "zombie laws" to take effect. Legislators need to listen to women who have been the victims of rape or incest. These are not voices that were given a fair hearing a hundred years ago.

Legislators need to listen to women today who know they are at greater risk of death from birth than from abortion. This is especially true for poorer women who have little or no access to prenatal care.

Legislators need to listen to physicians who need to struggle (now) with legal risks related to miscarriages that show up in an emergency room that might be either a miscarriage for natural reasons or the result of a botched attempt at self-abortion. Should legal self-interest interfere with providing necessary emergency care to these women? These physicians need to have a fair hearing today.

Legislators need to listen to couples who today would know they are at risk of having a child with a serious life-shortening genetic disorder. Such couples who have access to preimplantation genetic diagnosis can have a healthy child spared such life-diminishing risks, though multiple eight-cell embryos will have to be discarded to achieve that result. These are life-giving and life-affirming couples whose voices would be stifled by those "zombie" laws from the past. Legislators today have no right to be legislative zombies. They are politically obligated to engage their constituents in the present regarding appropriate and reasonable abortion legislation for which they can then be held accountable, whether at the state or federal level.

Finally, are reproductive rights safely entrusted to the political vagaries and ideological irrationalities that emerge in the states from time to time? How can it be reasonable with respect to reproductive rights and ordered liberty that obtaining a medical abortion at six weeks is a legally respected choice in one state while that same choice generates a criminal charge of murder in another? This is not a state of affairs that public reason can endorse, much less legitimate.

Notes

1. This paragraph was written in January of 2022. Since then, Politico released the majority opinion in this case as written by Judge Alito. www .documentcloud.org/documents/21835435-scotus-initial-draft This opinion is still subject to revision (it is labeled "1ˢᵗ Draft"), though the key conclusion, overturning *Roe* v. *Wade*, will likely stand. Space does not permit a lengthy analysis of this opinion. Alito criticized the Roe court for having "short-circuited the democratic process" (at 40), and for claiming the existence of a right to abortion that was not rooted in the nation's history and tradition (at 14). Alito endorsed Mississippi's claim that the State had an interest in protecting fetal life because this was "an unborn human being" and "some believe fervently that a human person comes into being at conception" (at 1). Finally, Alito contends the Roe decision was not consistent with "ordered liberty." What seems clear from Alito's opinion is that religiously rooted arguments are integral to the democratic process and may provide for the legitimate coercive imposition through state authority of laws that would constrain the liberal rights of some on the basis of religious beliefs not shared by those so affected. Permitting such outcomes does not seem congruent with equal rights in a liberal, pluralistic society. Further, it is difficult to imagine that "ordered liberty" would be preserved if public reason is not the foundation for that democratic deliberation. Instead, "disordered liberty," governed by prevailing political winds rather than stable commitments to rights, would be the result. Supporting this latter claim is one key objective of this volume.

2. Guttmacher Institute, 2021. It is worth recalling that Connecticut passed a law in 1879 that banned the use of any drug or device that furthered contraception. In 1964 Estelle Griswold, the director of a Planned Parenthood League in Connecticut, was arrested and fined $100 for giving advice on the use of contraceptives. The US Supreme Court overturned that law in *Griswold* v. *Connecticut* in 1965, affirming that married couples had a liberty right and a privacy right to buy and use contraceptives without government intervention (Oyez, 1965). Two things to note: This case, in affirming a privacy right as constitutionally protected, became the basis for a similar affirmation in *Roe* v. *Wade*. Secondly, the right in Griswold was affirmed only for married couples, a restriction that reflected more of a quasi-religious rationale than any public interest.

3. Michael Perry (1997) will defend, contrary to Rawls, the legitimacy of religious arguments in support of various pieces of controversial legislation, most especially regarding the moral permissibility of various practices (abortion, physician aid-in-dying) and the use of new medical technologies (preimplantation genetic diagnosis, the use of surrogate mothers). As an introduction to these debates, his book is very useful from a legal, constitutional perspective.

4. Wolterstorff, 2012.
5. Sanford Levinson (1992) writes: "Why doesn't liberal democracy give everyone an equal right, without engaging in any version of epistemic abstinence, to make his or her arguments, subject, obviously, to the prerogative of listeners to reject the arguments should they be unpersuasive (which will be case, almost by definition, with arguments that are not widely accessible or are otherwise marginal)" (at 2077)?
6. Christopher Eberle (2002) called attention to Bill McCartney, the Founder of Promise Keepers, who urged voters in Colorado to support Proposition 2, which would have permitted discrimination against homosexuals in many public venues, because he believed a homosexual lifestyle was "an abomination of almighty God" (at 4).
7. Rawls, 1996, at xxvii.
8. Rawls, 1996, at 3.
9. Rawls, 1996, at 9
10. Rawls, 1996, at 10.
11. Rawls, 1996, at 224.
12. Rawls, 1996, at liii.
13. Advocates for animal rights would dispute this sentence. However, that would represent one of those metaphysical beliefs that is beyond public reason.
14. Onyx Integrative Medicine, 2022.
15. Rawls, 1996, at 137.
16. Rawls, 1996, at 16.
17. Rawls, 1996, at 30.
18. Rawls, 1996, at 213.
19. Wolterstorff, 1997, at 105.
20. Vallier, 2012, at 157.
21. Berman, 2003.
22. Wolterstorff, 2012.
23. Wolterstorff, 2012, at 290.
24. Rawls, 1996, at 216.
25. Perry, 1988, at 181–82.
26. Quinn, 1997.
27. Quinn, 1995, at 49.
28. Vallier, 2012, at 150.
29. Greenawalt, 1995.
30. Schmidt and Babchuk, 1973.
31. Rawls writes, "And since the exercise of political power itself must be legitimate, the ideal of citizenship imposes a moral, not a legal, duty – the duty of civility – to be able to explain to one another on those fundamental questions how the principles and policies they advocate and vote for can be supported by the political values of public reason" (1996, at 217). We should be clear that picketing in these circumstances is an "exercise of political power." We need to ask, apart from education, what other jobs and professions would these picketers wish to ban gays from holding? Further,

what would be the political justification for such a ban? Prima facie, this represents a clear denial of equal concern and respect for gay individuals.

32. Rawls invokes this phrase to explain how there can be reasonable disagreement among individuals who are reasonable and rational, that is, committed to the relevance and necessity of public reason. Rawls sees this as part of "the ordinary course of political life" (1996, at 56). He gives several examples of the sort of things that can result in reasonable disagreement, including (1) empirical and scientific evidence that is conflicting and complex, (2) disagreement regarding the weight to be attached to specific norms or types of evidence, (3) the vagueness and indeterminacy of many of our moral and political concepts, especially as applied to hard cases, (4) the way individual experience may shape the interpretation of norms, and so on (1996, 56–57).

33. The discussion of "compassionate use" is linked with controversial "right to try" laws. The literature related to this discussion is substantial (Darrow et al., 2015; Jacob, 2015; Borysowski et al., 2017; Scharf and Dzeng, 2017; Mahant, 2020). In reviewing this literature, I have not found any specifically religious positions that have been taken regarding any side of this debate. However, strong libertarians have weighed in regarding "right to try" laws. Daniel Carpenter, a professor of government at Harvard, is quoted as saying, "The ultimate aim [of Goldwater libertarians] is a kind of libertarian paradise of deregulation" (Johnson, 2018). This libertarian perspective represents a comprehensive doctrine just as problematic from a public reason perspective as any strong religious perspective.

34. Eberle, 2002, at 20.

35. In much of the relevant literature produced by religious advocates there is a tendency to speak of secular reason as if it were equivalent to public reason. However, I am certain this is not an equivalence Rawls would endorse, in part because some range of comprehensive philosophic doctrines would be properly described as being part of secular reason. In that respect public reason cannot be identical with secular reason or nonreligious reason.

36. Swancutt, 2019.

37. Friberg-Fernros, 2015.

38. Lovering, 2012.

39. Simkulet, 2016.

40. Dworkin (1993) writes as follows: " ... .from the moment of conception a fetus embodies a form of human life which is sacred, a claim that does not imply that a fetus has interests of its own" (at 21). Dworkin believes the term "sacred" can be interpreted in a purely secular sense. He sometimes will use the term "inviolable" as a synonym for "sacred." Recall that Dworkin is writing as a political liberal.

41. Coastal Fertility Specialists, 2017.

42. Davis, 1995.

43. Dworkin, 1993.

44. Dworkin (1993) does claim that those two terms can be interpreted in a secular way. He also tends to speak mostly of fetuses rather than embryos, though he also asserts that these two properties apply from the moment of conception.

45. Rawls, 1996, at 58–66.

46. Unreasonable comprehensive doctrines are essentially forms of fanaticism. Fanatics see themselves as having "the whole truth," not only with respect to what to believe, but also with respect to how to live. Fanatics believe they have the right to use force to impose their views and policies on others. For fanatics there is no such thing as a reasonable compromise.

47. McCully, 2021.

48. Castelyn, 2020.

49. Hyun et al., 2021.

50. Blackshaw and Rodger, 2021.

51. Wolterstorff, 2012.

52. Rawls, 1999, at 490.

53. Rawls, 1999, at 578.

54. Rawls, 1996, at 137.

55. Wolterstorff, 2012, at 78.

56. Wolterstorff, 2012, at 81–82.

57. Wolterstorff, 2012, at 84.

58. Hancock et al., 2021.

59. Savulescu, 2001.

60. Parker (2007) is a critic of Savulescu's norm of procreative beneficence for practical, ethical, and conceptual reasons. He contends that "the interpretation of the duty to have the best possible child would emerge within intersubjective and socially embedded discourses about human flourishing and about what it would mean for a life to go well, and there is good reason to think that in any, even moderately, diverse community, no single, agreed concept of the best possible life is going to be possible or desirable."

61. Plant, 2009.

62. Plant, 2009, at 40.

63. Rawls, 1999, at 305.

64. Rawls, 1999, at 305.

65. Rawls, 1999, at 305.

66. Rawls, 1999, at 306.

67. Rawls, 1999, at 306. This is a 1980 essay by Rawls, "Kantian Constructivism in Moral Theory." As noted in the text, the quoted passages very much adumbrate the major themes on which Rawls elaborates in *Political Liberalism*.

68. The notion of reflective equilibrium may be seen as a technical concept in Rawls' political philosophy. However, it also has a common sense meaning and application. We want our moral and political lives to have a certain stability and coherence. We have to make decisions that require tradeoffs among competing values. Many reasonable trade-offs might be possible. But

all value trade-offs linked to policy options have practical implications and consequences, some of which represent future political problems or ethical challenges that could be avoided with the choice of a different tradeoff option. Rawls does not elaborate that much on how to interpret reflective equilibrium as a theoretical and practical methodology, but Norman Daniels (1996) does.

69. Engelhardt, 2017, at 11.
70. Cherry, 2017, at 86.
71. Cherry, 2017, at 89.
72. Cherry, 2017, at 90.
73. Fleck, 2021.
74. Hurlbut, 2015, at 128.
75. Hurlbut, 2015, at 115.
76. Hurlbut, 2015, at 115.
77. Hurlbut, 2015, at 128.
78. Hurlbut, 2015, at 128.
79. Rawls, 1996, at 127.
80. Quong, 2011 and 2014.
81. Lafont, 2009.
82. Miller, 2015.
83. DeMarneffe, 1994, at 235.
84. Quinn, 1995, at 43.
85. Eberle and Cuneo, 2015, section 6.
86. Quinn, 1995, at 42.
87. Quinn, 1995, at 44.
88. Quinn, 1995, at 44.
89. Greenawalt, 1988, at 12.
90. Rawls, 1996, at 225.
91. I suspect that I might be guilty of some oversimplified understanding of the world of mathematics. I respectfully request my mathematical readers to grant me some philosophic license.
92. Rawls, 1996, at 227.
93. Rawls, 1996, at 234.
94. Rawls, 1996, at 240.
95. Rawls, 1996, at 229.
96. Fleck, 2022.
97. Jones, 2020.
98. Lafont, 2009, at 144.
99. Quong, 2014.
100. Jiang, 2011. We should note that Steptoe and Edwards received the Nobel Prize for Medicine in 2011.
101. Kass (1997) can be seen as posing special challenges for public reason. He defends what he calls the "wisdom of repugnance." This has nothing to do with any religious perspective. Instead, he contends that the response of repugnance to cloning or artificial wombs or a number of other genetic technologies is sufficient to demonstrate that they are unethical. He calls

attention to incest as something that elicits repugnance, which means for him that no additional argument is needed to justify that conclusion.

102. DeClercq and Zephyrin, 2021.
103. Smajdor, 2007.
104. See also Cavaliere (2020) and MacKay (2020) for arguments in support of the artificial womb as a technology that can support greater political equality for women. Tim Murphy (2012) is one of Smajdor's critics. She replies to his article in that same journal issue (2012).
105. Thompson, 1971.
106. There is obvious room here for considerable contentiousness. Anencaphalic infants would clearly satisfy this condition, as well as infants with holoprosencephaly or comparable gross brain deformities. Fetuses with Trisomy-13 or Trisomy-18 might satisfy this condition, given multiple congenital problems and very short life expectancies. Trisomy-21 would be more problematic, though many parents today choose abortion in this circumstance.
107. Rasanen, 2017.
108. Mathison and davis, 2017.
109. Blackshaw and Rodger, 2019.
110. Kaczor, 2018.
111. Hendricks, 2018.
112. Segers et al. (2020) raise the issue of the fetus as a patient in this essay, given the artificial womb option, though they ultimately want to give greater weight to the autonomous decisions of the mother, at least in the case of partial gestation in the artificial womb.
113. Kendal, 2020.
114. Romanis (2018) wants to argue that the fetus in the artificial womb is neither a baby nor a fetus. She suggests referring to it as a "gestateling." She also rejects my suggestion that the artificial womb might be thought as an extension of the NICU. She sees the artificial womb as something that "replaces a natural function rather than facilitating a newborn rescue" (at 755). She does agree with me that this requires reconsideration of what we might have regarded as settled ethical and policy judgments regarding this entity. She introduces the terminological change to signal that need.

A Provocative Postscript

1. All the quoted materials are from the first five pages of the *Dobbs* opinion, which is referred to as "the syllabus."
2. Rawls, 1996, *Political Liberalism,* 231–40.
3. We noted previously Alito's assertion that a right to abortion was not an "essential component" of ordered liberty. What makes something an "essential component" of ordered liberty? Rights of free speech, assembly, a free press, freedom to petition the government, and religious liberty would all seem to be essential components for maintaining a liberal, democratic society. These are also integral elements of public reason. How is it that gun

rights belong in this listing before reproductive freedom rights? This is incoherent. See also: Editorial Board. The Supreme Court Puts Gun Rights above the Human Life. *New York Times* (June 25, 2022). https://www.nytimes.com/2022/06/25/opinion/supreme-court-gun-control-bill.html

4. This phrase comes from the Mississippi law that was being challenged in *Dobbs*. It is intended to cover the entire period from conception to birth. See 597 US section I (2022).

5. See 597 US section II C 1 (2022). See also 597 US section II D 3 (2022).

6. Alito writes, "Our opinion is not based on any view about if and when prenatal life is entitled to any of the rights enjoyed after birth" (p. 38). This statement strikes me as disingenuous since later in that same paragraph Alito condemns those who would "regard a fetus as lacking even the most basic human right—to live." Also, earlier in the text Alito recounts all the laws outlawing abortion from the middle of the nineteenth century to the middle of the twentieth century. He seems perfectly accepting of all those laws that would charge someone with murder who provided access to abortion. Such a charge only makes legal sense if the fetus is believed to have a right to life.

7. Caroline Kitchener and Devlin Barrett. Antiabortion lawmakers want to block patients from crossing state lines. *The Washington Post* (June 30, 2022). https://www.washingtonpost.com/politics/2022/06/29/abortion-state-lines/

8. See 597 US section II B 2 a (2022).

9. See 597 US section III A (2022).

References

Berman, Paul. 2003. "The Philosopher of Islamic Terror." *New York Times Magazine* (March 23). www.nytimes.com/2003/03/23/magazine/the-philosopher-of-islamic-terror.html

Blackshaw, Bruce P., and Daniel Rodger. 2021. "Why We Should Not Extend the 14-day Rule." *Journal of Medical Ethics* 47: 712–14.

Blackshaw, Bruce P., and Daniel Rodger. 2019. "Ectogenesis and the Case Against the Right to the Death of the Foetus." *Bioethics* 33: 76–81.

Borysowski, Jan, Hans-Jorg Ehni, and Andrzej Gorski. 2017. "Ethics Review in Compassionate Use." *BMC Medicine* 15: 136–43.

Castelyn, Grant. 2020. "Embryo Experimentation: Is There a Case for Moving Beyond the 14-day Rule?" *Monash Bioethics Review* 38 (2): 181–96.

Cavaliere, Giulia. 2020. "Gestation, Equality, and Freedom: Ectogenesis as a Political Perspective." *Journal of Medical Ethics* 46: 76–82.

Cherry, Mark. 2017. "The Scandal of Secular Bioethics: What Happens When the Culture Acts as if There is No God?" *Christian Bioethics* 23 (2): 85–99.

Coastal Fertility Specialists. 2017. "Why do Chromosomally Normal Embryos Not Implant in the Uterus?" www.coastalfertilityspecialists.com/resources/blog/why-do-chromosomally-normal-embryos-not-implant-in/ Accessed 3/23/22.

Daniels, Norman. 1996. *Justice and Justification: Reflective Equilibrium in Theory and Practice*. Cambridge: Cambridge University Press.

Darrow, Jonathan J., Arneet Sarpatwari, Jerry Avorn, and Aaron Kesselheim. 2015. "Practical, Ethical, and Legal Issues in Expanded Access to Investigational Drugs." *New England Journal of Medicine* 372: 279–86.

Davis, Dena S. 1995. "Embryos Created for Research Purposes." *Kennedy Institute of Ethics Journal* 5 (4): 343–54.

Declercq, Eugene and Laurie Zephyrin. 2021. *Severe Maternal Morbidity in the United States: A Primer*. The Commonwealth Fund (October). www.commonwealthfund.org/publications/issue-briefs/2021/oct/severe-maternal-morbidity-united-states-primer#:~:text=Each%20year%2C%20as%20many%20as,avoided%20with%20timely%2C%20appropriate%20care. Accessed 4/3/22.

DeMarneffe, Per. 1994. "Rawls's Idea of Public Reason." *Pacific Philosophical Quarterly* 75: 232–50.

Dworkin, Ronald. 1993. *Life's Dominion: An Argument About Abortion, Euthanasia, and Individual Freedom*. New York: Knopf.

Eberle, Christopher. 2002. *Religious Conviction in Liberal Politics*. Cambridge: Cambridge University Press.

Eberle, Christopher and Terence Cuneo. 2015. "Religion and Political Theory." *Stanford Encyclopedia of Philosophy*. https://plato.stanford.edu/archives/spr2015/entries/religion-politics/. Accessed 4?30/22.

Engelhardt, H. Tristram. 2017. *After God: Morality and Bioethics in a Secular Age*. Younkers: St. Vladimir's Seminary Press.

Fleck, Leonard M. 2022. *Precision Medicine and Distributive Justice: Wicked Problems for Democratic Deliberation*. New York: Oxford University Press.

Fleck, Leonard M. 2021. "Alzheimer's and Aducanumab: Unjust Profits and False Hopes." *Hastings Center Report* 51 (4): 9–11.

Freeman, Samuel (ed.). 1999. *John Rawls: Collected Papers*. Cambridge, MA: Harvard University Press.

Friberg-Fernros, Henrik. 2015. "A Critique of Rob Lovering's Criticism of the Substance View." *Bioethics* 29 (3): 211–16.

Greenawalt, Kent. 1995. *Private Consciences and Public Reasons*. New York: Oxford University Press.

Greenawalt, Kent. 1988. *Religious Convictions and Political Choice*. New York: Oxford University Press.

Guttmacher Institute. 2021. "Abortion Policy in the Absence of Roe." www.guttmacher.org/state-policy/explore/abortion-policy-absence-roe Accessed 1/20/2022.

Haberman, Clyde. 2014. "Baby M and the Question of Surrogate Motherhood." *New York Times* (March 23). www.nytimes.com/2014/03/24/us/baby-m-and-the-question-of-surrogate-motherhood.html Accessed 4/3/22.

Hancock, Susan, Katherine Taber and James Goldberg. 2021. "Fetal Screening and Whole Genome Sequencing: Where are the Limits?" *Expert Review of Molecular Diagnostics* 21 (5): 433–35.

Hatch Egg Donation & Surrogacy. 2022. "The Best U.S. States for Surrogacy in 2022." www.hatch.us/blog/best-worst-states-for-surrogacy Accessed 3/31/22.

Hendricks, Perry. 2018. "There is No Right to the Death of the Fetus." *Bioethics* 32: 35–97.

Hurlbut, Benjamin J. 2015. "Religion and Public Reason in the Politics of Biotechnology." *Notre Dame Journal of Law, Ethics, and Public Policy* 29: 101–28.

Hyun, Insoo, Annelien Bredenoord, James Briscoe, Sigal Klipstein, and Tao Tan. 2021. "Human Embryo Research Beyond the Primitive Streak." *Science* 371 (6533): 998–1000.

Jacob, Julie A. 2015. "Questions of Safety and Fairness Raised as Right-To-Try Movement Gains Steam." *JAMA* 314: 768–60.

Jiang, Lijing. 2011. "Robert Geoffrey Edwards and Patrick Christopher Steptoe's Clinical Research in Human In Vitro Fertilization and Embryo Transfer, 1969-80." *The Embryo Project Encyclopedia* (May 12). https://embryo.asu.edu/pages/robert-geoffrey-edwards-and-patrick-christopher-steptoes-clinical-research-human-vitro Accessed 4/3/22.

Johnson, Stephen. 2018. "Is the New 'Right to Try' Law Libertarian Quackery or Lifesaving Hope?" *Politics and Current Affairs* (May 31). https://bigthink.com/politics-current-affairs/trump-signs-right-to-try-bill-that-lets-the-terminally-ill-take-experimental-drugs/ Accessed 3/20/22.

Jones, Bradley. 2020. "What is a Super Responder?" *Cancer Today* (June 26). www.cancertodaymag.org/Pages/cancer-talk/What-is-a-Super-Responder.aspx Accessed 3/31/22.

Kaczor, Christopher. 2018. "Ectogenesis and a Right to the Death of the Prenatal Human Being: A Reply to Rasanenr." *Bioethics* 32: 634–38.

Kass, Leon. 1997. "The Wisdom of Repugnance: Why We Should Ban the Cloning of Humans." *The New Republic* 216 (22): 17–27.

Kendal, Evie. 2020. "Pregnant People, Inseminators and Tissues of Human Origin: How Ectogenesis Challenges the Concept of Abortion." *Monash Bioethics Review* 38: 197–204.

Lafont, Cristina. 2009. "Religion and the Public Sphere: What Are the Deliberative Obligations of Democratic Citizenship?" *Philosophy & Social Criticism* 35 (1–2): 127–50.

Levinson, Sanford. 1992. "Religious Language and the Public Square." *Harvard Law Review* 105 (8): 2061–79.

Lovering, Rob. 2012. "The Substance View: A Critique." *Bioethics* 27 (5): 263–70.

Mackay, Kathryn. 2020. "The 'Tyranny of Reproduction': Could Ectogenesis Further Women's Liberation?" *Bioethics* 34: 346–53.

Mahant, Vijay. 2020. "'Right to Try' Experimental Drugs: An Overview." *Journal of Translational Medicine* 18: 253–59.

Mathison, Eric and Jeremy Davis. 2017. "Is There a Right to the Death of the Foetus?" *Bioethics* 31: 313–20.

McCully, Sophia. 2021. "The Time has Come to Extend the 14-day Limit." *Journal of Medical Ethics* 47: e66. http://doi.org/10.1136/medethics-2020-106406.

Miller, Eric C. 2015. "The Drama of American Religious Freedom." *Politics and Religion* 8: 818–25.

Murphy, Timothy J. 2012. "Research Priorities and the Future of Pregnancy." *Cambridge Quarterly of Healthcare Ethics* 21: 78–89.

Onyx Integrative Medicine. 2022. Naturopathic Treatment Approach. https://onyxintegrative.com/is-a-naturopathic-doctor-a-real-doctor/ Accessed 2/02/2022.

Oyez. 1965. *Griswold v. Connecticut*. 381 US 479 (1965). www.oyez.org/cases/1964/496 Accessed 1/20/ 2022.

Parker, Michael. 2007. "The Best Possible Child." *Journal of Medical Ethics* 33 (5): 279–83.

Perry, Michael J. 1997. *Religion in Politics: Constitutional and Moral Perspectives*. New York: Oxford University Press.

Perry, Michael J. 1988. *Morality, Politics, and Law*. New York: Oxford University Press.

Plant, Raymond. 2009. "Citizenship, Religion, and Political Liberalism." In *Religious Voices in Public Places*, edited by Nigel Biggar and Linda Hogan. New York: Oxford University Press, 37–57.

Quinn, Philip L. 1997. "Political Liberalisms and Their Exclusions of the Religious." In *Religion and Contemporary Liberalism*, edited by Paul J. Weithman. Notre Dame: University of Notre Dame Press, 138–61.

Quinn, Philip L. 1995. "Political Liberalisms and the Exclusions of the Religious." *Proceedings and Addresses of the American Philosophical Association* 69 (2): 35–56.

Quong, Jonathan. 2014. "On the Idea of Public Reason." In *A Companion to Rawls*, edited by Jon Mandle and David Reidy. Oxford: Wiley Blackwell, 265–80.

Quong, Jonathan. 2011. *Liberalism Without Perfection*. New York: Oxford University Press.

Rasanen, Joona. 2017. "Ectogenesis, Abortion and the Right to the Death of the Fetus." *Bioethics* 31: 697–702.

Rawls, John. 1996. *Political Liberalism*. New York: Columbia University Press.Rawls, John. 1999. *Collected Papers*. Edited by John Freeman. Cambridge: Harvard University Press.

Romanis, Elizabeth Chloe. 2018. "Artificial Womb Technology and the Frontiers of Human Reproduction: Conceptual Differences and Potential Implications." *Journal of Medical Ethics* 44: 751–55.

Savulescu, Julian. 2001. "Procreative Beneficence: Why We Should Select the Best Children." *Bioethics* 15: 413–26.

Scharf, Amy and Elizabeth Dzeng. 2017. "'I'm Willing to Try Anything': Compassionate Use Access to Experimental Drugs and the Misguided Mission of Right-To-Try Laws." *Health Affairs* (March 27). www.healthaffairs.org/do/10.1377/forefront.20170327.059378/ Accessed 3/2/22.

Schmidt, Alvin J. and Nicholas Babchuk. 1973. "The Unbrotherly Brotherhood: Discrimination in Fraternal Orders." *Phylon* 34 (3): 275–82.

Segers, Seppe, Guido Pennings, and Heidi Mertes. 2020. "The Ethics of Ectogenesis-Aided Foetal Treatment." *Bioethics* 34: 364–70.

Simkulet, William. 2016. "A Critique of Henrik Friberg-Fernros's Defense of the Substance View." *Bioethics* 30 (9): 767–73.

Smajdor, Anna. 2011. "In Defense of Ectogenesis." *Cambridge Quarterly of Healthcare Ethics* 21: 90–103.

Smajdor, Anna. 2007. "The Moral Imperative for Ectogenesis." *Cambridge Quarterly of Healthcare Ethics* 16: 336–45.

Swancutt, Katherine. 2019. "Animism." *Cambridge Encyclopedia of Anthropology*. www.anthroencyclopedia.com/entry/animism Accessed 3/21/22.

Thomson, Judith Jarvis. 1971. "A Defense of Abortion." *Philosophy and Public Affairs* 1: 47–66.

Vallier, Kevin. 2012. "Liberalism, Religion and Integrity." *Australasian Journal of Philosophy* 90 (1): 149–65.

Vallier, Kevin. 2011. "Against Public Reason Liberalism's Accessibility Requirement." *Journal of Moral Philosophy* 8: 366–89.

Williams Jeremy. 2015. "Public Reason and Prenatal Moral Status." *The Journal of Ethics* 19(1): 23–52.

Wolterstorff, Nicholas and Robert Audi. 1997. *Religion in the Public Square: The Place of Religious Convictions in Political Debate*. Lanham: Rowman and Littlefield.

Wolterstorff, Nicholas. 2012. *Understanding Liberal Democracy: Essays in Political Philosophy*. Edited by Terence Cuneo. New York: Oxford University Press.

Acknowledgments

My deepest thanks to Tomi Kushner for unlimited encouragement and practical advice regarding this manuscript. My thanks to Tim Murphy for many helpful conversations regarding the status of embryos, in addition to his related published work. My thanks to Marleen Eijkholt for calling my attention in the literature to the notion of gestatelings. Finally, enormous thanks to Jean Edmunds, my partner in life and love and labor, for astute attention to editing details.

Cambridge Elements ≡

Bioethics and Neuroethics

Thomasine Kushner

California Pacific Medical Center, San Francisco, USA

Thomasine Kushner, PhD, is the founding Editor of the *Cambridge Quarterly of Healthcare Ethics* and coordinates the International Bioethics Retreat, where bioethicists share their current research projects, the Cambridge Consortium for Bioethics Education, a growing network of global bioethics educators, and the Cambridge-ICM Neuroethics Network, which provides a setting for leading brain scientists and ethicists to learn from each other.

About the Series

Bioethics and neuroethics play pivotal roles in today's debates in philosophy, science, law, and health policy. With the rapid growth of scientific and technological advances, their importance will only increase. This series provides focused and comprehensive coverage in both disciplines consisting of foundational topics, current subjects under discussion and views toward future developments.

Printed in the United States
by Baker & Taylor Publisher Services